"An excellent and useful book,
The Temples of London reads like a good novel
at a fast pace, covering the historical roots
and the modern and relevant –
just like the mayoralty."
— *The Rt Hon Fiona Woolf, CBE,
Lord Mayor of London 2013–14*

"A super read"
– *London Historians*

The TEMPLES
of LONDON

Roger Williams

Other books by Roger Williams

Non-fiction
The Fisherman of Halicarnassus
The Royal Albert Hall: a Victorian Masterpiece
for the 21st Century
London Top 10
The Most Amazing Places to Visit in London (*co-author*)
Royal London (*illustrations by John Cleave*)
Eyewitness Barcelona and Provence
Berlitz Dubrovnik and Tenerife
& many other travel books and guides

Fiction
Aftermath
A-Train
Burning Barcelona
Father Thames
High Times at the Hotel Bristol
Lunch with Elizabeth David
All fiction titles are available as ebooks

Father Thames was the winner of the 2013 SAFTA
(Southwark Arts Forum) Award for Literature.
"A beautifully written collection of London stories"
– Jerry White
"Exemplary stuff"
– The Londonist

"You can build a temple to anything
that's positive and good."

– *Alain de Botton*

Published in the UK by Bristol Book Publishing
www.bristolbook.co.uk

The Temples of London
ISBN: 978-0-9567416-8-4

Typeset in Plantin and Trade Gothic
Printed and bound in the UK by
TJ International Ltd, Padstow, Cornwall

The TEMPLES
of LONDON

The TEMPLES of LONDON

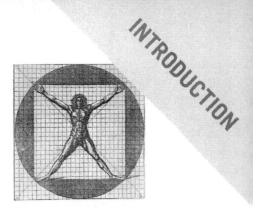

THE STARTING POINT OF ALL ARCHITECTURE

What do St Paul's Cathedral, the British Museum and the Bank of England have in common? They are all built in the Classical style, based on pagan temples of antiquity. London is full of porticos great and small, with pillars, pediments and allegorical figures decorating religious, civic, industrial and domestic buildings. For hundreds of years inspiration from ancient Greece and Rome became set in stucco and stone, and it is hard to walk down a city street without encountering elements of their influence. Even the most daring modern architects maintain a backward glance towards the roots of their discipline.

The Pritzker Prize, the 'Nobel of Architecture', is awarded each year to the world's top practitioner at locations that have included the Palace of Versailles, the People's Palace in Beijing and Philip Hardwick's Classical Goldsmiths' Hall in London. It comes along with $100,000 and a gold medallion inscribed *firmitas, utilitas, venustas* – 'strength, utility, beauty'. These three virtues of architecture were set down in the 1st-century BC by Vitruvius, the Roman author of *De architectura*. His ten-volume book is the only surviving work on the subject from antiquity. Relating buildings to the human figure, he matched perfection in architecture with perfection in nature, illustrating the ideal human body with outstretched arms and legs touching the edges of both a perfect circle and a perfect square. Quoting many Greek examples and precedents, Vitruvius created a language for buildings, cataloguing the Classical orders of Doric, Ionic and Corinthian, and he took the temple as the starting point, the *template*, of all architecture.

Roman Londinium's only surviving temple ruin is the Temple of Mithras, which dates from the 2nd century AD. Now returned to its original site near Cannon Street station, it is overshadowed by much newer temples, for there are many kinds of temples and many kinds of gods, and one of them is the 'false god of greed' called Mammon. Temples, it seems, are everywhere. In fact, according to St Paul, there may be around eight million walking, talking temples in London: *"Know ye not that your body is the Temple of the Holy Ghost which is in you?"* he admonished the Corinthians.

My body is a temple... Holy, inviolate, invaluable, inspirational, a temple is a handy metaphor that can serve a host of purposes.

"Wikipedia is a temple of the mind," Jimmy Wales, founder of the online encyclopedia, told the *Observer*.

"You can build a temple to anything good," Alain de Botton, author of *Religion for Atheists: a Non-Believer's Guide to the Uses of Religion,* said at the launch of his book in 2012.

Among de Botton's proposals for temples to abstract, non-religious ideas was a 150ft (46m) Temple to Atheism, or Temple to Perspective, which would rise in the midst of the City of London's financial skyscrapers. The initial design by Tom Greenall shows the Earth's life, each millimetre of height representing a million years, and a thin band of gold a metre from the ground vividly making the point that, in terms of the universe, human existence is insignificant.

De Botton is happy for everyone to have their own beliefs, unlike the revolutionaries of France and Russia who turned religious houses into museums and temples of atheism. When Notre Dame Cathedral in Paris became the Jacobins' Temple de la Raison, statues of the Virgin and the saints were replaced by images of the Age of Reason's evangelists, Rousseau and Voltaire, who had predicted that within a hundred years of his death the only place anybody would be able to find a Bible would be in an antiquarian book shop.

Were he alive today, more than two hundred years later, Voltaire would have to look to his reasoning, because worldwide annual sales for Bibles are around 100 million copies. In London there are many other sacred texts for sale, too, from the different faiths whose religious houses have added to the city's rich mix of buildings. Attendance at Anglican churches may be low, but among many other communities congregations are growing. Figures for 2012 show church attendance overall in the capital had risen by sixteen percent in just seven years.

Diverse beliefs have created such a collection of buildings around the city in recent decades that to visit them is to go on a cultural world tour. Some must make do with makeshift premises, while the better endowed have settled in large estates just outside the capital, from the Mormon Temple near East Grinstead in Surrey to the Gurdwara Sri Guru Singh Sabha in Southall, the largest Sikh temple in Europe.

Other inspired and venerated buildings, temples to their patrons and to their purposes, celebrate the arts and sciences, triumphing a multitude of achievements. Among them are some of London's greatest institutions. They give their devotees somewhere to gather to sing their praises and to radiate the messages of their beliefs. *Firmitas, utilitas, venustas*: strong, useful and beautiful, their fabric is borne up by solid faith.

THE CITY SKYLINE

In 2011 **New Court**, Rothschild Bank's latest headquarters, was completed in St Swithin's Lane. This typically sunless City street is barely 150 yards long and so narrow that it is difficult to appreciate the frontage of any building. But what Dutch architects Rem Koolhaas and Ellen Van Loon of the Office of Metropolitan Architecture (OMA) did was to raise the building's skirts, as it were, so that a vista opened up between two glass-box legs to reveal the churchyard of **St Stephen Walbrook** beyond. The church is one of Sir Christopher Wren's finest, a precursor to St Paul's Cathedral, with a 64ft (20m)-high dome and a spire of around 120ft (37m), and this new view of its east end brings welcome light into the lane.

Above its two legs, the cubic glass tower of OMA's New Court rises to a rooftop garden, by which time the church's copper dome and Classical spire are way below. Perched higher still above the garden is the Sky Pavilion, two storeys of glass that act as a periscope. In this celestial Panorama Room Rothschild's Wealth Management directors and their guests can raise their gaze beyond the parish churches and look visitors stepping out onto the Golden Gallery above the dome of St Paul's Cathedral directly in the eye.

Once the loftiest of institutions, the Christian Church seems earthbound now, but New Court shows that high-flying financiers can still show it some respect. A symbiotic relationship keeps City institutions and religious houses embraced, matching material support with the prospect of spiritual redemption, but while they are in each other's clutches they have to compete for air. There are around forty churches in the City's Square Mile, which until a century ago was made up of more than a hundred parishes, reflecting the number of churches that existed before the 1666 Great Fire of London. No other secular patch on Earth has such a concentration of religious houses, and though they may seem like woodland flowers among the forest of skyscrapers, these ancient buildings owe their continued existence to their benefactors: the guildsmen, merchants and financial powerbrokers of the City.

N.M. Rothschild has been on the St Swithin's Lane site since Nathan Mayer arrived from Frankfurt via Manchester, starting his banking business here in 1805. This is where, three years later, his son Lionel, the first Jewish Member of Parliament, was born. An enlarged painting and tapestry, plus a collection of the bank's old metal trunks are in a window display to hint at the family's long residence and illustrious past as key financier of the Napoleonic wars and bullion broker to the Bank of England.

St Stephen Walbrook is nothing if not a history lesson, too. Originally Saxon, it was one of some fifty churches rebuilt by Charles II's Royal Surveyor, Sir Christopher Wren, after the Great Fire. Beneath the beautiful dome is an 8.5-ton circular block of travertine marble that serves as an unusual, central altar. Carved by Henry Moore, its soft indentations make it appear as pliable as putty, but it is supposed to reflect the Dome of the Rock on Temple Mount in Jerusalem, where Abraham was prepared, on God's instructions, to sacrifice his only son, prefiguring the crucifixion.

This bold implant, which caused great controversy, was commissioned during a ten-year restoration programme begun in 1978 under property developer Peter Palumbo, the Arts Minister in the government of Margaret Thatcher, who rewarded him with the title of Baron Palumbo of Walbrook. He is also responsible, with the architect James Stirling, for the nearby candy-striped post-modern **No. 1 Poultry** opposite **Mansion House**. In the 1960s Palumbo, who has owned houses built by Frank Lloyd Wright and Le Corbusier, had been refused permission to install a Mies van der Rohe skyscraper block on the six-acre site that had been acquired by his property-developer father Rudolph, the son of Italian immigrants who ran a café in Lower Thames Street. Getting in his way was the 1870 neo-Gothic flagship of the Crown Jeweller, Mappin & Webb, by the London architect John Belcher. But in 1994, he finally had permission to pull it down, along with a clutch of listed buildings, to put up Stirling's jazzy office block.

No. 1 Poultry has a smart rooftop restaurant, the Coq d'Argent, with a terrace from which four city workers in five years have jumped to their deaths. Just a few yards away in St Stephen Walbrook is the telephone of the world's first helpline (dial MANsion House 9000; today 08457 909090), installed here in 1953 when the Samaritans, a non-religious service 'for suicidal and despairing people', was set up by the rector, Dr Chad Varah. But the casualties of No. 1 Poultry never made the call.

Always an attraction, rooftop views pose a security problem as well as a health and safety risk. IRA bombs put paid to the rotating restaurant on the **BT Tower** in 1971 and closed the observation deck of Canary Wharf Tower in 1996. Post-9/11 security is even tighter, but views remain an enormous attraction. Europe's tallest building when completed in 2012, Renzo Piano's **Shard** arrived with predictions that in its first year it would have a million visitors to its viewing platforms, despite the high price of tickets. And the Sky Garden, open to the public on the top of the '**Walkie-Talkie**' at **20 Fenchurch Street**, may placate critics who think the 32-storey building that widens as it grows taller is simply overbearing.

Some views of London are sacrosanct, most notably of St Paul's Cathedral, which at 365ft (111m) is one-third the height of the Shard. An Act of Parliament keeps the view clear from as far away as King Henry's Mound in Richmond Park ten miles to the west. The Palace of Westminster and the Tower of London are similarly protected.

The legislation is an important buffer against the upward rush of skyscrapers and it is continually being challenged. Technological developments of glass and metals, of computer software and 3D modelling, combined with a constant need to attract global financial players, has brought a clutch of exceptional buildings. These are mostly confined to the City's southeast district of EC3, between Bishopsgate and Aldgate, where they compete with buildings of every age like eager contestants in a talent contest frantically shouting, "*Look at me, look at me!*"

One of the first, in the mid-1980s, was the **Lloyd's**

Building, a startling innovation by Richard Rogers. Fresh from the Centre Georges Pompidou, the Paris triumph he shared with the Italian Renzo Piano, he broke new ground in the City with this building that wore its insides outside and eliminated office barriers by creating a large central atrium to ease internal communications. It was courageous, even heretical, of Lloyd's, and like no previous temple to Mammon.

Reflecting on his achievement, Rogers said, "Today's buildings are more like evolving landscapes than Classical temples in which nothing can be added, and nothing can be removed."

Rogers was born in Florence and spent the first half dozen years of his life in Italy before the family came to England. His father's grandfather, an English dentist, had settled there, and his mother, a ceramicist, came from Trieste. Ernesto Rogers, a cousin, was a successful architect in Italy, and after the war Richard spent time in his office. Dyslexia and lack of drawing skills were no bar to his education, which took him to Yale where James Stirling was a visiting tutor. A fellow student was Norman Foster, a Mancunian from a working-class background who shared Rogers' enthusiasm for Frank Lloyd Wright and high-tech. Back in London they formed, with their then wives Su Brumwell and Wendy Cheeseman, a practice called Team 4.

The partnership did not last but these two modern builders of Mammon's temples have boxed and coxed throughout their long careers. In 2008 Foster would shove the 28-storey **Willis Building** in the face of Lloyd's in Lime Street, which by then had been given a Grade I listing, turning it, ironically, into a temple in which nothing can now be altered. Rogers replied with the **Leadenhall Building** (the Cheese Grater), which overshadowed Foster's **30 St Mary Axe** (the

Gherkin). Both enobled architects set up their practices by the Thames, Rogers in the former Duckham's oil wharf in Fulham where his wife Ruth's Riverside Café has its own devotees, while architects often drop in on Foster + Partners' modern studio where a 180ft (60m) wall of glass looks out on to the Thames beside the Battersea campus of the Royal College of Art. Both have chosen their titles from the river: Baron Rogers of Riverside and Baron Foster of Thames Bank.

It is the River Thames that shows off London's architecture to best effect. The rich mix of buildings raised beside it for God and Mammon is unequalled anywhere in the world. London mayors have always knelt at the feet of anything tall, and from their office in Norman Foster's wobbly egg-shaped **City Hall** they have taken inspiration from the skyline of the Lord Mayor's City of London opposite. EC3's unique achievements line up along the 800 yards between London Bridge and Tower Bridge. In this fifteen-minute stroll, every sort of turret, tower, column, spire, and rooftop from the past one thousand years jostles for attention.

By London Bridge station, the Shard acts like a giant gnomon, casting its shadow across the water and stretching as far as the Barbican at midday on the winter solstice. As the sun arcs behind it, a shady finger sweeps west to east, pointing out the buildings of EC3 one by one: the Egyptian Art Deco of **Adelaide House** (John James Burnett, which when completed in 1925 was the tallest office block in the city, with a golf course on the roof); 1,000-year-old **St Magnus the Martyr**; Christopher Wren and Robert Hooke's **Monument** (the tallest free-standing stone column in the world, 1677); the Brutalist block of **St Magnus House**, with a public terrace on the third floor overlooking the river (Richard Seifert, 1978); the deep blue glass of the **Northern & Shell** building (Covell Matthews, 1985); the golden fish weather vanes of the neo-Renaissance **Old Billingsgate Market** (City architect Horace Jones, 1875); Robert Smirke's neoclassical **Customs House** (1825); the spire of Samuel Pepys' **St Olave**; and the medieval **Tower of London**. Seen just behind are late 20th-century silhouettes: Lloyd's arched roof (Richard Rogers, 1986); the Art Deco lines of **One America** (RHWL, 1990); and the zany pink Gothic of **Minster Court** (GMW Partnership, 1991). Looming larger still are the 21st-century steel-and-glass contributions: **Heron Tower** and the much delayed **Pinnacle** or Helter Skelter (both Kohn Pederson Fox); Foster's Gherkin; Rogers' Cheese Grater; and Rafael Viñoly's top-heavy 20 Fenchurch Street, or Walkie-Talkie, which one sunny September day in 2013 managed to melt parts of an expensive Jaguar XJ and a Vauxhall Vevaro van with solar reflection from its concave mass of glass.

Problems can be expected on technology's cutting edge, but a similar thing happened to a Viñoly building in 2010 when plastic bags and cups melted and the swimming pool warmed in his Las Vegas Vdara hotel. The Uruguayan-born architect has a number of buildings in Britain to his credit but when it came to working in the City, it seems he was unprepared.

"I didn't realise London would be so hot," said Viñoly.

With luck the weather will have been factored in to his designs for the Battersea Power Station masterplan, which will create another architects' showcase on London's river.

THE TEMPLE OF MITHRAS

The first time the exterior of **St Stephen Walbrook** could be appreciated from a suitable distance was at dawn on Sunday May 11, 1941 after London had suffered the worst air-raid of the war. On that deadly moonlit night 1,438 had been killed and 1,800 injured, and many of London's major buildings were damaged or destroyed. The Lord Mayor's parish church was among the casualties, but because the area around it was reduced to rubble, it was suddenly bathed in full sunlight for the first time in hundreds of years.

With a plain façade and a small front porch beside a square bell tower, the church never looked particularly grand, and it had long been cramped among its surrounding. Before **Mansion House** was built, there was a Stocks Market on the north side where Wren planned a splendid portico for his church, but the daily stench from the meat and fish stalls put paid to the idea, leaving a modest exterior that gave no hint of its interior grace.

The original AD700 Saxon church dedicated to St Stephen, the first Christian martyr, stood a few yards away on the site of a Roman **Temple of Mithras** on the west bank of the Walbrook river, but in the 15th century, funded by the Grocers' guild, it was moved to the east bank in order to sever its pagan roots, though by this time the river had been driven underground. The temple was then forgotten until 1955 when the site was finally cleared of the wartime bomb debris to build **Bucklersbury House**, a fourteen-storey headquarters for the Legal & General insurance company. This was the tallest office building of its time and the first to break through the 100-feet height restriction.

No Roman temple had been discovered in London before, and people queued to see it.

Architectural ideas imported from Greece and Rome came with their gods who were forever blowing in from the east like gathering clouds, picking up local deities along the way. Hovering in the heavens over Britain, they mingled with their Celtic hosts, listening to the rising prayers, pleas and curses, and looking down on sacrifices and libations. The east is where life arose with the sun, and where all mysteries began. Altars faced east; people were buried with their feet towards the east. Roman London soaked up Egyptian Isis and Serapis, Anatolian Cybele and Persian Mithras. Superstition prevented the Romans from ignoring the gods of the tribes they conquered, and they simply absorbed them. If the Celtic god of war was called Camulos, he must be the same god they called Mars, and so temples were erected to Mars-Camulos. These conciliatory arrangements, could never be countenanced by monotheists.

Religious sites often occupy former hallowed ground, and who knows what mystic copse or clearing topped Ludgate Hill where a Temple to Diana (Greek Artemis) is thought to have stood and where three cathedrals dedicated to St Paul of Tarsus have since been raised. There may have been an earlier henge here, and there are rumours of a ley line passing through.

The Roman temple from which St Stephen Walbrook developed was dedicated to Mithras, a late Roman solar deity of Indo-Persian origin, picked up by the troops of Alexander the Great in his foray into the Indian subcontinent and transported west by legionaries from the Macedonian empire's eastern frontiers. A heroic figure, Mithras is depicted single-handedly slaughtering a bull. His manly cult became an exclusively male club, a freemasonry of army officers, administrators and businessmen who met to back-scratch and perform their Mysteries. Their temples were distinctive, and often underground, representing the cave in which Mithras had dragged a bull for its sacrifice. Followers were baptised with water and they drank the blood of slaughtered bulls. Born from a rock, Mithras is sometimes depicted dining with the sun god, Sol, and banqueting seems to have been part of the celebrants' rituals.

After the temple had been uncovered, it was partially removed under the direction of the Museum of London and placed ninety yards away in Queen Victoria Street so that it could remain on public view and building development could take place. As the new block rose, so St Stephen Walbrook once more slid into the shadows. Half a century later, however, the west front of the church once again saw the full light of day when Bucklersbury House came down and a gaping hole opened in preparation for the building of **Bloomberg Place**, a new European headquarters for Bloomberg L.P.

Michael Rubens Bloomberg, three times mayor of New York, philanthropist, wire service provider and magnate of Mammon, had announced that his company had outgrown City Gate House in Finsbury Square, a former gentlemen's club designed by Giles Gilbert Scott, which it had occupied since 2001. Foster + Partners, who had added a modern block to the building, drew up plans for the new site, where Foster was just completing another large project, The Walbrook office block.

Bloomberg Place stands astride the Temple of Mithras's original site on the banks of the River Walbrook which, at Bloomberg's expense, has been excavated by archaeologists prior to the temple being returned to its foundations. The Walbrook had been key to the Roman settlement of London. Running in a valley between Ludgate Hill and Cornhill, it provided fresh water at a favourable point on the tidal, marshy Thames, and this is where the Romans built their port. Bucklersbury House marked the approximate spot of the upper limits of navigation, just above the Roman governor's house. Water was associated with Celtic gods, and votive offerings were tossed into rivers along with hopes and prayers. Rivers were rubbish dumps, too, and the damp sediment helped to preserve myriad artefacts.

Archaeological digs generally go out to tender, with museums, universities and institutions bidding for the contract. But Bloomberg wanted the finds for his own Foundation, so he shelled out for the excavation, and fifty archaeologists from the Museum of London Archaeology began clawing through the three acres of mud in what would soon be Bloomberg Place. Searching through the former banks of the river turned out to be like panning for gold. Some 13,000 Roman trinkets and other artefacts were collected, the earliest from AD43. Sophie Jackson, project manager of the excavation, said: "We're calling this site the Pompeii of the North."

All their finds now belong to Bloomberg L.P. to be viewed along with the Temple of Mithras inside the building, which is scheduled to open in 2017. However, MOLA points out that, customarily, developers donate artefacts to local museums when the analysis of them is complete. In this case they are expected to end up in the **Museum of London**.

The Mithras finds will always be a reminder of the largesse of Michael Rubens Bloomberg, one of the top ten richest men in America. He has given away billions of dollars to a variety of causes, and his stated ambition is to "bounce the cheque to the undertaker". The new London building, restricted to ten floors because of St Paul's Cathedral's protected sightlines, will also be the headquarters of his charitable Bloomberg Foundation, and when he is here, the former New York mayor will be able to look down on another Roman temple. Or, rather, a building that looks like a temple: **Mansion House**, the Palladian home of London's Lord Mayor. Designed in the mid-18th century by George Dance the Elder, its grand portico has six Corinthian columns and a pediment with the triumphant figure of the City of London. The main reception room, which can be seen on the regular weekly tours, is the magnificent Egyptian Hall, which is Dance's idea of how a palace on the Nile might look.

The Lord Mayor of London takes up residence here each November for his, or her, year in office, and as he looks up at the new glass box beside him, he may well compare himself to his New York counterpart. The job of the American mayor comes with a salary of around $220,000 a year, as opposed to the Lord Mayor who has no salary at all. While it is true that Michael Bloomberg declined his wages, demanding only a token dollar a year for his work, he did spend $73 million of his own money in his campaign to secure the post. The Lord Mayor, by comparison, has no election expenses, as he is simply chosen from among the City's aldermen, but during his year of office he must spend around 100 days abroad promoting the City, and he personally pays for all the wine that is served to guests at Mansion House, his old-fashioned home.

MAMMON GOES EAST

From below, **Canary Wharf Tower**, properly called **One Canada Square**, seems to taper upwards, like an obelisk or a stele made from a single bar of steel, ending in a pyramid on which a guiding red light twinkles and smoke escapes like burning incense. Obelisks were built at the entrance to temples, acting as a rallying point, and the Tower, dating from the 1980s, was a call to the City's finance houses. Around it, the builders of the new age of glass and steel would begin scraping the East London sky.

The brains behind the Docklands developments was the pixie-faced reclusive Canadian Paul Reichman and his brothers Albert and Ralph, with their company, Olympia and York. Based in Toronto, they knew about cold winters and underground malls. They knew how to build heavenwards, too, initially hitting the heights with First Canadian Place, a skyscraper for the Bank of Montreal that occupied a city block and was the tallest in the country. After that came the World Financial Center on a landfill site in Battery Park in downtown New York, which has become something of a tourist destination. Then on to Canada Wharf in London, which reoriented the whole city eastwards. Although they would later undergo several reverses of fortune, these developments made the Reichmans, and Olympia and York, the world's largest private landlords.

The docks had been closed for seven years when Olympia and York stepped in, taking over a 28.5 hectare site on the Isle of Dogs, the peninsula on a broad meander in the River Thames. The West India Docks' three basins cut through the peninsula's throat to make it more like an island, and the development began by sinking a mall beneath the intended Tower in the central Export Dock. Canary Wharf took its name from a wharf on West Wood Quay where bananas from the Canary Islands were landed by the Norwegian Fred Olsen's Fruit Lines. It seems to be mere coincidence that the Romans knew the Atlantic archipelago as Canaria Insula, the Isle of Dogs, and that it was on the Canary Island of Tenerife that Fred Olsen helped Thor Heyerdahl to set up the Kon Tiki Museum, which sets out the ocean explorer's theory that the island's ancient pyramid structures were introduced by the Egyptians who stopped here on their way to central America.

These pieces of information would have been of no consequence to the developers, though ventilation buildings and service sheds in front of Canary Wharf Tower have distinctly ancient Egyptian echoes. Maybe there was just something in the air.

For the initial development Reichman turned once again to César Pelli who had masterminded the World Financial Center, and they would go on to build the breath-taking Petronas Twin Towers in Kuala Lumpur. Born in Argentina, Pelli had been Dean of the School of Architecture at Yale University prior to the Canary Wharf project. What he brought to the totemic Tower was stainless steel, an expensive metal that gets its bling from added chromium. The metal that gave New York's Art Deco Chrysler building its sheen had been used by Pelli in the World Financial Center. It was a feature of Rogers' Lloyd's Building, too, but the Canary Wharf Tower was given a full metal jacket. Panels of specially made steel were hung on an aluminium frame, reflecting light and turning the whole building gold in the late afternoon sun. Inside, a steel pendulum known as a 'tuned mass damper' was installed to hold the 770ft (235m) building steady should high winds cause it to sway beyond 13 inches (33mm).

The metal's clean lines in the Tower are complemented by an interior of shiny surfaces in marble, stone, slate and glass. All the subsequent buildings in the development are spacious and so sharp edged that they can only have been created by computer. In reality, Canary Wharf can look like an architect's drawing, sketched in with workers in well pressed suits and skirts, and no sign of grey hair or children.

Reichman and Pelli created the form. Michael von Clemm followed with the function. He is the man credited with setting the spark to make Canary Wharf London's finance centre. The charismatic if autocratic New York entrepreneur banker and pioneer in Euromarkets is one of those financiers around whom many stories are spun. A professor of anthropology, he spoke Swahili, dressed impeccably, loved food and gave the Roux brothers money to start La Gavroche, a favour returned when they named their Chelsea restaurant La Tante Claire after his aunt. As chairman of Credit Suisse First Boston Bank, he saw in Canary Wharf the kind of potential that had been fulfilled on the waterfront in Boston where he had briefly worked as a crime reporter, and though he backed out of direct investment with Olympia and York, he saw the site as providing the 'back office' for banks. In other words, this was where they would do all their dealing away from the expensive property in the Square Mile. This was just after the Big Bang in 1986, when banks were deregulated and electronic trading replaced the bear pit of the Stock Exchange floor. Prestigious City buildings that had been designed to impress customers no longer had a place. What mattered most was having staff and software working around the clock to gamble on the increasingly fast and complex world money markets. There was no space for the encumbrance and clutter of history.

Major banks, abandoning their handsome City headquarters, would leave their pasts behind, trading in descriptive addresses – Cheapside, Threadneedle Street, Crutched Friars – for simple, numbered blocks. One bank in Bishopsgate, however, was ahead of the rest and made the move upwards before making the move eastwards. That was the National Westminster Bank, which put up the City's first real skyscraper in 1981. The architect of the **NatWest Tower** was Richard Seifert, and he is credited with introducing the high-rise aesthetic into Britain's cities, notably in 1966 with Harry Hyam's **Centre Point**. Notoriously kept empty for many years for tax reasons, it did nothing to help give property developers a good name.

Seifert was born in Switzerland where his father was a doctor, grew up in London and insisted on being addressed by his wartime rank of 'Colonel'. It was said that he shaped London's skyline more than anyone since Christopher Wren, and that he was the first architect to become a millionaire. In London alone he was responsible for several hundred buildings, from the Royal Gardens Hotel in Kensington to Euston Station, which replaced Philip Hardwick's neoclassical original. An example of the Colonel's handiwork could be seen from the fifth floor of any London building, it was once claimed.

Seifert was adept in his dealing with local planners, and for his NatWest scheme he obtained permission to pull down Philip Hardwick's **City of London Club**. At the last minute, however, it was given a reprieve by the City Corporation, allowing it to survive as the oldest gentlemen's club in the Square Mile, with Prince Philip as its patron. Seifert was also refused permission to demolish the old bank building's handsome 19th-century Italianate Banking Hall, designed in 1865 by John Gibson. Its landmark frontage on the corner of Bishopsgate and Threadneedle Street has unmissable statues and friezes by John Hancock, and until 2013, when it was announced that it would become a hotel, it could be hired for functions.

The tallest building in Europe at the time was occupied by the bank for just fifteen years before being sold. In 2000 the National Westminster Bank was bought by the Royal Bank of Scotland and their London headquarters are now at 135 Bishopsgate, a come down from what has become **Tower 42**, named after Seifert's forty-two-storey building. It now has multi-occupancy and a rooftop restaurant, and most of its lessees are not directly involved in banking.

RBS has a strong presence in Canary Wharf where, in 2007 at the start of the global financial crisis, they sold **25 Canada Square** in a whopping £1.1billion deal. Designed by Pelli, this is one of the twin skyscrapers beside Canary Wharf Tower. The other is **8 Canada Square,** headquarters for the 8,000 staff of HSBC, by Norman Foster, who attached a smaller building to Pelli's tower to create the Citigroup Centre.

This central trio of Docklands buildings are said to have been designed to look like an upturned three-pin plug. Whether this is true or not, Canary Wharf is Mammon's Milky Way, its electric lights twinkling brightly through the night. If the steel and glass can be, as Pelli suggested, a portal to the sky, reflecting clouds and sunlight during the day, then the buildings at night are also heaven-sent. Who needs outer space anyway, when such star-gazing can be had here on earth? In stark contrast, many of the neighbouring apartment blocks in Docklands, bought as investments, lie in the darkness of deep space.

Beneath Canary Wharf Tower is Cabot Square, the axis of the original development. The piazza is centred on a fountain at the start of a boulevard heading due west towards the Thames. On either side are warmer and more familiar brick- and stone-clad buildings from Skidmore Owings & Merrill, with Classical touches. If Gianlorenzo Bellini's colonnaded arms around the sides of St Peter's Square in the Vatican have suggested the embrace (or claws) of the Roman Catholic church, the arms of Cabot Square have had the same effect, drawing the money-makers into this new metropolis.

Of all people, Paul Reichman knew the Bible's injunction that God and Mammon must not mix. Work was never allowed at his developments on the Sabbath, and Christian as well as Jewish holidays were respected. No place of worship has been built at Canary Wharf, although a Multi-Faith Prayer

Room has been tucked in behind Waitrose. There is also a floating church, the only one in London, permanently moored in the North Dock opposite the Museum of London Docklands. Bought in Holland and sailed here in 2003, **St Peter's Barge** has a full-time team of four, administered by the parish of St Anne in Limehouse.

Canary Wharf may be without religion, but it is not without superstition. Gambling requires luck. It is not uncommon for skyscrapers not to have a 13th floor, and Canary Wharf Tower is no exception. Chinese dragons also bring good fortune, and the pair that were familiar symbols of HSBC in China were copied to guard the bank's Canary Wharf building.

The original bronze lions were commissioned from the sculptor Henry Poole to protect the front door of the 1923 neoclassical Hong Kong and Shanghai Bank building in Shanghai. One roaring, one watchful, they were nicknamed Stephen and Stitt after managers whose personality they seemed to reflect. In 1946 the bank moved its headquarters to Hong Kong and the lions are now in the Shanghai Museum.

A second pair was commissioned for the Hong Kong building, and their noses and teeth were still being touched for luck when Norman Foster built a new headquarters on the island in 1985. Foster had lost out to Rogers over the Lloyd's commission, and this was his response: a spectacularly innovative building, hung between two internal towers, and the world's costliest commercial project to date.

In designing the new building Foster had to hire the services of a necromancer to ensure that its *feng shui* attracted positive *chi* energy forces and repelled negative ones. Few people in Britain were then aware of this ancient Chinese science. Translated as 'wind water', the elements considered to be life's two most vital forces, *feng shui* had been the sacred knowledge of a few chosen masters, handed down father to son throughout Chinese history. It affected every aspect of the home as well as the building of Taoist temples and the planning of whole cities. Early Christian missionaries had encountered it when they were dissuaded from erecting crosses because it was bad *feng shui* to 'stab the land'. Suppressed under communism, particularly by the Red Guard who viewed it as feudalistic superstition, it remained something of a closely guarded secret.

Foster's encounter with *feng shui* seemed to let the genie out of the bottle. Reports began to circulate about how, under the necromancer's spell, HSBC's Hong Kong lions had been specially orientated, the bank's escalators had been designed to represent the whiskers of a dragon to suck in money, and rods had been installed on top of the building to repel negative forces from the rival Bank of China. Suddenly there was a raft of stories in the British press about *feng shui*. Home and style magazines sought advice and considered its effects on interior design, room layout and colour schemes. Businesses started to think about it, too, and today many major international organisations take *feng shui* into account when organising their offices.

Canary Wharf itself has excellent *feng shui*. Water is the main source of money luck and the River Thames is the water dragon, the life force of London. Coming from the west along with the prevailing wind, it creates positive energy that accumulates in 'the nest of the dragon', and within that nest is the inward meander of the river where the *chi* settles. This is the 'belly of the carp' in the City of London, and it is here that the *chi* comes ashore. But one of the problems with *chi* in the City is that its buildings are all higgledy-piggledy, with front doors facing different directions allowing no clear paths for the energy forces to enter. This is the result of the City growing up organically, with no grid or master plan. *Chi* does not like anything messy.

Continuing east, the energy forces reach a great meander in the Thames at Limehouse, and, leaving the river, head straight down the boulevard into the 'armchair *feng shui*' of Cabot Square. Here the trio of buildings – Canary Wharf Tower, HSBC and CitiCorp – conform to the three halls or towers of a Taoist temple. By supporting the workers in the main Tower, Pelli and Foster's twin buildings ensured they were no longer isolated, and the resulting configuration attracted further investment into the area.

This must be what makes the banks here so successful. When J.P. Morgan moved into their new offices in 2012, Canary Wharf overtook the City to become the largest banking district in Europe.

THE CRUSADERS' LEGACY

Health and safety laws in Britain dictate that every large public gathering, from football matches to state occasions, must have a proportionate number of first-aid practitioners on hand. This service is provided by the Red Cross and, in Scotland, by St Andrew First Aid. But the overwhelming number comes from St John Ambulance, the country's leading supplier of first-aid training. A familiar sight in their uniforms with white cross insignias, this volunteer organisation seems a long way from the crusading Knights Hospitaller, whose ancient buildings they occupy and from whom they took their name.

The **Hospital of St John** is thought to have been founded in Jerusalem in 1078 by merchants from Amalfi in Italy, under the blessed Gerard Tum. The millennium had spread fear throughout Christendom that the world would soon end, sparking a rush for redemption through pilgrimages to the Holy Land, which had been in Muslim hands for nearly 400 years. To care for them, Gerard administered the best of Christian, Jewish and Islamic medical practice in a hospital he set up next door to the **Church of the Holy Sepulchre**, which the pilgrims had all come to see, since this was not only believed to be where Christ was crucified but also where he had been entombed.

Twenty-one years later, in 1099, the First Crusaders took Jerusalem for Christendom. Expelling the existing Eastern Orthodox Patriarchs and setting up a Latin Patriarch beholden only to the Pope in Rome, they made their headquarters in the Al-Aqsa Mosque on Temple Mount, and this would become the palace of their new Christian Kingdom of Jerusalem. On this pivotal Biblical spot, thought to be the location of Solomon's Temple, two French knights, Hugues de Payens from Champagne and Godfrey de Saint Omer from Picardy, founded The Poor Fellow Soldiers of Christ and of the Temple of Solomon to guard and protect the city and its pilgrims. The Knights Templar, as they were more succinctly called, were sanctioned as a religious order under the Augustinian rule of poverty, chastity and obedience, and their emblem was a red cross, which was emblazoned on their white mantles. In 1129 Hugues de Payens returned to Europe to secure the blessings of the Templar Order from the Pope and the abbot of Clairvaux. He also visited England to found the Order in London.

Following in their footsteps, the Hospitallers of St John were reorganised as a religious order under Gerard's successor, Raymond de Puy, and a few years afterwards they took on a military role to become fighting monks. Though the two organisations, as well as the third, the Germanic Teutonic Knights, would become bitter rivals, initially they worked together, and they began to rebuild the Church of the Holy Sepulchre. They repaired the rotunda, constructed a century earlier by the Patriarch of Byzantium above the cave in which Christ is supposed to have been buried. An ambulatory, chancel and a grand south entrance were added, and the church was rededicated in 1149, a crowning moment at the end of the Second Crusade.

By now land and gifts were being showered on the knights' organisations all across Europe, and on these estates they built their houses, or preceptories, where young men would be trained to become crusaders. The Templars' European headquarters was established in Paris in the 30-acre fortified Enclos du Temple, which was enclosed behind a 26ft (8m)-high wall. Their round churches would encourage worshippers to think of the Church of the Holy Sepulchre in Jerusalem.

In London, following the visit of Grand Master Hugues de Payens, a round Templar church, known as the **Military**, or **Old Temple** was built at the top of Chancery Lane near Staple Inn. Meantime the Knights of St John acquired a 10-acre site half a mile away in Clerkenwell. It had been given to them in 1144 by an Anglo-Norman landowner, Jordan de Briset and his wife Muriel de Munteni, and here they established a convent and **Priory of St John** with a round church.

The Military Temple, built of Caen stone, was in use for no more than two decades, after which the Templars decamped to the site known today as **Temple**, between Fleet Street and the Thames. It is unclear why they made this move, but it must have offered better opportunities, and perhaps the church of St John, to which a chancel had been added, had eclipsed their own and they wanted something bigger. Stones from the Military Temple, of which nothing remains, may have been used to build the **New Temple Church** by the river.

Both the New Temple and the Priory Church of St John were dedicated in February 1185 by Heraclius, the French-born, Italian-educated Latin Patriarch of Jerusalem. The Second Crusade had failed to consolidate gains in the Holy Land, and the Patriarch had arrived in England in the hope of persuading Henry II to keep a promise made to the Pope that he would lead a crusade to Jerusalem as a penance for the murder of the Archbishop of Canterbury, Thomas Becket. With him was Roger de Moulins, Grand Master of the Hospitallers. The Templar Grand Master, Arnold of Tottoja, had died en route to England, in Italy.

The dedication of the two churches was an unprecedented state occasion. Henry II, who spoke only Latin and French, was surrounded by his court, judged the richest in Europe. Many of the knights, as their remains in the church have revealed, topped six feet, and their mantles were uniforms that commanded the greatest respect. Enjoying enormous prestige and not yet tainted with any division or scandal, their joint procession was a high point of their history in London. At their head was Patriarch Heraclius, a bejewelled potentate crowned with a glittering mitre and carrying souvenirs and relics of the Holy Land as well as the key to the city of Jerusalem. Never mind that he was rumoured to have been chosen only for his looks, and was known to run a harem.

However, Henry II, with enough trouble at home, refused all entreaties to lead a crusade, and two years later Jerusalem was retaken by Saladin. In 1189 Henry's son, Richard I, the Lionheart, led the English contingent on the Third Crusade, in which knights wore the white cross of the Hospitallers, while those from France, under Philip II, the red cross of the Templars. Teutonic Knights, white crosses on black, never reached the Holy Land: they lost heart half way there when their leader, the 68-year-old Holy Roman Emperor Frederick Barbarossa, fell off his horse and drowned in a river in Anatolia.

The Crusade made some gains but failed to take Jerusalem, and in subsequent reverses the Knights fell back first on Cyprus and Rhodes, which the Hospitallers ruled as a sovereign state, then Malta, where they continued to protect pilgrims and harass Muslim shipping. The island would remain their headquarters for nearly three hundred years, adopting the eight-pointed cross as its emblem.

The Templars did not last half as long. The knights' vows of poverty enriched the movement, as they often bequeathed their property to the Order, while pilgrims would leave their money for safe keeping before embarking on their journey, with a note to reclaim funds at their destination, but of course many never reached the Holy Land let alone completed the round trip. Royalty and the Pope began to rely on the Orders for loans. In London, the Temple enclosure included cloisters, an ecclesiastic court and administrative centre as well as residences for Templar monks and knights, with exercise grounds for the military and their horses. English kings were among its guests, and, according to the chronicler Matthew Paris, Roman pontiffs would stay when they came to extract "unheard of extortions of money and valuables".

In debt and jealous of their wealth, Philip IV of France determined to close the Order down, and he managed to convince the Pope of its heresy and greed. Inquisitors began their tasks, and in 1314, two years after the organisation was dissolved by the Pope, the last Grand Master, Jacques de Morlay, was executed in Paris.

The Pope granted all Templar property to the Knights of St John. In England they took over the Templar land by the Thames, which included two halls that served as refectories for the knights and the priests. It was around these two buildings that the **Inner** and **Middle Temple** were to develop as inns of court for two societies of lawyers who rented it from the Hospitallers. History here has a gap, because the lawyers' paperwork was a target of the Peasants' Revolt of 1381, which also saw the Priory of St John in Clerkenwell set on fire. The Prior, Robert Hales, who had served the Order on a number of crusading missions, was also the king's treasurer and collector of the poll tax. He was taken to Tower Hill by the mob and beheaded. The Priory burned for a week.

Recovering from the set-back, the Order of St John survived and prospered up until the Reformation. Its estates included what is now St John's Wood in north London as well as a large granary and farm on which Hampton Court Palace would be built. Despite this, and the fact that Henry VIII had enjoyed hospitality at Clerkenwell and taken the Grand Master with him to France for the great gathering of European knights at the Field of the Cloth of Gold, the Priory was a target of the Tudor king's attack on the Church of Rome. It was the last great religious house in the country to be dissolved.

As the Priory broke up and declined it passed through various hands but it did not entirely disappear. The Priory South Gate, now **St John's**

Gate, was the main entrance on the north side of Smithfield market. Rebuilt in 1504, it is one of London's oldest buildings. Here the poor and needy once gathered for handouts. Known as Jerusalem Passage, until the First World War it housed a pub called the **Jerusalem Tavern**, and although the nearby Jerusalem Tavern in Britton Street looks ancient, it in fact dates only from 1996.

The Hospitallers' story is told in a museum inside St John's Gate where there are portraits of the grand masters, a model galley, arms, and the silver plates from which the sick would be fed. It also has displays on the story and activities of the St John Ambulance service.

On the north side of the Gate is the cut-down priory church, which was given to St John Ambulance in 1932 by the Church Commissioners when the congregation had diminished. The round church had been demolished at the beginning of the 14th century, and its site is described in an arc of cobblestones in St John's Square in front of what remains of the priory church, while segments of its foundations can be seen in the crypt. Paintings and banners hang from the otherwise bare walls of this large, flat-roofed hall where rows of chairs are set out for use by representatives of St John Ambulance from around the country, each one labelled for a particular division.

A small, secluded cloister garden planted with herbs that the Hospitallers would have gathered to tend the sick, lies beside the church, and is a quiet place for a lunchtime sandwich.

Meanwhile, driven from Malta in 1798 by Napoleon, who tore down the Enclos du Temple in Paris, the Catholic Sovereign Military Hospitaller

Order of St John of Jerusalem, of Rhodes and of Malta re-established itself in Rome. Variations of the Order had existed in northern Europe since the Reformation, and 19th-century causes – Greek irredentists, Carlist absolutists – from time to time encouraged eccentric characters to brandish their swords in the name of these chivalric orders.

In Britain, the Order of St John resurfaced as a charitable, non-religious organisation to combat injury and disease wreaked by the industrial revolution, offering first-aid training in factories and workplaces as well as in the home, and in 1874 the Knights of St John were made an Order of Chivalry once more by Queen Victoria. It was then that they also acquired St John's Gate. St John Ambulance also re-established links with Jerusalem by opening an eye hospital in the city. Serving east Jerusalem, Gaza and the West Bank, it continues its charitable work there.

Spread mainly through the Commonwealth, there are around 400,000 St John Ambulance volunteers worldwide, serving forty-two countries. They are often first on the scene in disasters and conflicts. Lack of religious belief is no bar to signing up. The Duke of Gloucester is the Grand Prior, and Nelson Mandela is among notable figures to have been made a Bailiff Grand Cross of the Order.

Internationally, the Red Cross, symbol of the Knights Templar, is far better known, and has nearly 100 million volunteers. The papacy has almost, but not completely, apologised for accusing the Templars of heresy, and Dan Brown's 2003 book, *The Da Vinci Code,* brought a new interest in the Order, putting the Temple Church and this quiet corner of the city firmly on the tourist map. The Temple's good fortune has been to have ended up in the care of lawyers, whose wealth and influence have ensured the preservation of this enclave that remains outside the jurisdiction of both the City and the Bishop of London.

The Round Church, a two-tiered drum, was built at the moment of transition between Romanesque and Gothic, and though much restored, it remains an attractive building. It has an elaborate Norman west doorway, a nave was added in the 13th century, Wren produced battlements and the Victorians gave it a substantial makeover. It was rebuilt after being bombed in the war when the effigies of knights on their tombs were disfigured, but fortunately casts had already been made and they can be seen in the Victoria and Albert Museum. Despite these ravages of history, the church still seems an ancient place. It has excellent acoustics, and it supports two professional ensembles, the Temple Singers and Temple Players, as well as the resident Temple Church Choir.

The Middle Temple is an atmospheric enclosure, its alleys cobblestoned, gas-lit and full of the ghosts of London's past. It has the air of an ancient university, which to some extent it is, and there are many rare books and manuscripts in its extensive library. Its gardens are well maintained, particularly the large lawn going down to the Thames, open to the public on weekday lunchtimes, while Fountain Court, with a giant mulberry tree by the pool, is an idyll. Between Fountain Court and the Round Church is **Middle Temple Hall**, the most handsome Elizabethan building in London, with a rare double hammerbeam roof and Shakespearean connections. *Twelfth Night* was first performed here, and a timber from Sir Francis Drake's *Golden Hinde* is given a ceremonial use when lawyers are called to the bar.

The hall also has one of the Temple's biggest secrets, one far more practical than any clues about the Holy Grail. During term time, if it is not being used for functions, Middle Temple Hall is open to any reasonably dressed visitor, who may lunch here.

SABBATH IN THE CITY

Saturday mornings in the City are a quiet time. The bankers, merchants and wheeler-dealers are home with their families, or they have left for the country, or perhaps they are getting their golf bags packed. Shops and coffee bars are closed, traffic is light and the streets are free from all but the more adventurous tourists. So the figures who emerge in suits and Sunday best from Aldgate tube station stand out. With a sense of purpose they walk past the wooden mock City gate erected for the Olympics and head down Duke's Place to **Bevis Marks**, where they pass through an arch with wrought-iron gates to enter the courtyard of Britain's oldest synagogue.

Bevis Marks was not a famous Jew, though when some people first learn of the synagogue they think he must have been. The oldest unaltered religious house in the City bears the same name as the street. A long while before the synagogue was built, the Abbey of Bury St Edmunds had property here, its boundaries identified by its 'marks', and the name is thought to be a corruption of Bury's Marks. In fact the synagogue isn't called Bevis Marks at all. Its proper name is Sha'ar ha-Shamayim, meaning Gate of Heaven.

Some synagogues in America are called temples,

but in Europe they are all just synagogues. Most Jewish sects believe that there is only one temple, the one that is waiting to be rebuilt on Temple Mount, or Mount Zion, in Jerusalem on the coming of the Jewish Messiah. The original building is thought to have been the work of King Solomon in the 10th century BC, which was destroyed by the Babylonian king Nebuchadnezzar II in 587BC when the Jews went into exile. On their return seventy years later a second temple was built by Herod the Great and this in turn was destroyed by the Romans in AD60. Since the 7th century Temple Mount has been occupied by the Al-Aqsa Mosque and Dome of the Rock.

At first sight, the interior of Bevis Marks looks surprisingly like other City churches and reflects the buildings of the time. This was just after the Great Fire of London, when Charles II's master architect, Sir Christopher Wren, was in charge of the rebuilding. The king had returned to re-establish the monarchy after Oliver Cromwell had overseen the execution of his father and installed a republic. Cromwell promoted religious freedom, allowing Jews to settle for the first time since they had been expelled from England some three hundred years earlier. Some say that Cromwell was so deeply religious himself that he feared the Messiah's Second Coming might be imminent and he would suffer hellfire if he did not show tolerance. But of course there was politics involved, and these were not economic migrants. They were wealthy merchants from Amsterdam.

These first arrivals were Sephardim, descendants of Jews from the Iberian peninsula who two centuries earlier had been driven out, along with the Moors, first from Spain, then Portugal. There was no sign of the synagogue and ghetto their predecessors had built in Old Jewry beside Guildhall, and the new arrivals did not venture far from Aldgate, the eastern gate, beyond which they bought a patch of land for burying their dead.

Sephardic Jews spoke Ladino, a language akin to medieval Spanish. Following the diaspora in Roman times, they had headed west from Israel across the Mediterranean and North Africa to arrive in Spain. Other Jews had wandered north into Eastern Europe to become the Yiddish-speaking Ashkenazim. Ashkenazi Jews were poorer, though more numerous, than the more aristocratic Sephardim. Their synagogue was built around 1690 in Duke's Place, which is in fact the same short thoroughfare as Bevis Marks, a street that changes names again at Camomile Street as it heads northwest to Bishopsgate. Until the Second World War, the **Great Synagogue** in Duke's Place was the largest in the City.

The first synagogue to be purpose-built for the Sephardim had been established in Creechurch Lane in 1657. Perhaps spurred on by the arrival of the Ashkenazim, the Portuguese and Spanish Jewish Congregation found funds to build the handsome synagogue in Bevis Marks street in 1701, based on the one they had left behind in Amsterdam. They could have asked for a temple more fitting to their faith, but at this time of unprecedented church building in London, it was easier to negotiate with someone who had the contacts and local expertise to put up a church, and, besides, the new immigrants were anxious to fit in. The builder they appointed was a Quaker, Joseph Avis, who had worked on Wren's St Bride's. Apparently, he refused his fee, saying it was wrong to profit from building a house to God. Little else seems to be known about Avis, so perhaps his magnanimous gesture was his undoing.

Built along the pure, unadorned lines of English Baroque, Bevis Marks included features that reflected Amsterdam's much bigger Esnoga, the Ladino word for synagogue, built some twenty-five years earlier and still in use today. The Amsterdam congregation even donated the largest of the seven chandeliers that represent the days of the week, while the faux-marble pillars are the same number, twelve, as the tribes of Israel. The focal point is the Echal or Arc, which contains the scrolls of the five books handed to Moses. With fluted columns and gilded Corinthian capitals, it would not look out of place as an altarpiece in an Anglican church. The male congregation sits in facing rows of oak seats, with locked boxes for their personal belongings beneath, and there are also several benches brought here from the earlier synagogue in Creechurch Lane. A later addition is the choir, something the Amsterdam Esnoga does not possess. Women are confined to the latticed gallery, where the benches are even more uncomfortable, though the windows make it a light and airy space. Glass cabinets here contain a collection of Torah mantles, some cut down from wedding gowns. The oldest is from 1720, made of lace-patterned silk with panels of velvet and silver gilt that belonged to Moses Lopes Pereira, who had amassed his fortune in Vienna where he had been a favourite of the Empress Maria Theresa who made him First Baron Aguilar.

Better-known names associated with the synagogue include the prime minister Benjamin Disraeli, whose family were congregants, and its notable benefactors, Moses Montefiore and the

Rothschilds. The chair nearest the Arc, which Montefiore occupied, is kept for special visitors, such as incoming Jewish Lord Mayors, who walk here from Mansion House for Sabbath eve prayers immediately after being elected.

It is a miracle that the building was never damaged during the Second World War. The much larger Great Synagogue of the Ashkenazim in Duke's Place was completely destroyed during the night of the Sabbath on May 10, 1941, in the bombing raid that devastated London and would lead to the discovery of the Temple of Mithras. The Great Synagogue was the third building on the site, designed in 1795 by George Dance the Elder, architect of Mansion House. A temporary building was erected and used until 1958, by which time most Jewish families had moved out of the area, to north and west London, and it was never rebuilt.

Although it survived the war, Bevis Marks Synagogue suffered damage from the two IRA bombs that rocked the City in 1992 and 1993, first at the Baltic Exchange then, on a spring Sabbath, in Bishopsgate, where a truck-load of explosives was detonated, damaging the synagogue's roof and windows. The truck had been parked outside the Hong Kong and Shanghai Bank and the massive explosion caused more than a billion pounds' worth of damage. The NatWest Tower was badly affected and the quaint medieval church of St Ethelburga, which had been a rare survivor of the Fire of London, collapsed. A telephone warning from the IRA kept casualties low, but a photographer was killed and more than forty were injured.

Today, Bevis Marks sees itself as the Cathedral Synagogue of Anglo-Jewry. It is popular for special occasions, such as weddings, when candle light enriches the patina of ages on the woodwork, and the brass chandeliers and wall lamps gleam gloriously. But its regular congregation is small, and there are rarely more than forty or so at Sabbath services. To counter this, it has added early morning weekday prayers. This is designed to attract some of the thousands of Jewish City workers, a number of them from overseas, before they start their toil in the nearby temples of Mammon.

THE GRAND TEMPLE

*"He shall build me a house and I will
establish his throne for ever."*

This was the command handed down from God to
Solomon, King of Israel, for the building of the First
Temple on Temple Mount in Jerusalem. The words
are taken from the Bible (1 Chronicles 17:12) and
they are inscribed alongside the figures of Solomon
and Hiram on the ceiling of the Grand Temple in
the **Freemasons' Hall** in Great Queen Street,
Covent Garden.

The Phoenician King Hiram of Tyre aided in the
building of Solomon's temple, supplying cedar wood
and expertise, but the ceiling figure that holds the
Square and Compasses symbol of the masons is
ambiguous because there is another biblical Hiram
who is essential to the Freemasons' Craft. Hiram
Abiff was King Hiram's great builder, "filled with
wisdom and understanding and cunning to work all
works in brass" and he was sent to oversee the
Israelites' thirteen-year construction programme in
Jerusalem. According to the first Book of Kings,
which gives a detailed description of the First Temple,
'stonesquarers' cut the stones so perfectly that they

fitted together without need of mortar. The Bible does not, however, include the story of Hiram's murder one night while building the temple. According to this story, he was attacked by three workers who wanted to discover the secrets of the mason's trade, so that they too could become master builders and thus command a higher wage. Struck by each one in turn, Hiram refused to give up his secrets, and he died from a blow from a maul inflicted by the third assailant. This story is at the core of the Freemasons' movement, and it is enacted in plays learned by heart by members as they progress through their third degree of initiation.

No archaeological evidence has yet come to light to prove the existence of Solomon's temple, but its biblical testimony is potent enough to have produced the Freemasons' magnificent Grade II* listed **Grand Temple**. The building lies at the heart of the Freemasons' Hall that commemorates members killed in action during the First World War. As the headquarters of the United Grand Lodge of England, it is the only surviving Art Deco building in London still used for its original purpose. Solid Italian marble pillars, lapis lazuli pavements, gilt inlays, mahogany panelling, brass lamps and stained glass embellish the interior rooms that spread across two and a quarter acres, encompassing a grace-and-favour accommodation, library, museum and twenty-one additional 'temples' and meeting rooms.

The Grand Temple is on the first floor of the central part of the complex that extends into a void, an airy moat separating it from the surrounding building. As a result, no external sound penetrates the walls. It is a place of utter silence with perfect acoustics, and its lack of internal pillars or columns means that sight lines are unrestricted, a selling point that is emphasised to anyone who wants to hire the hall. It has provided an ideal setting for productions of *The Magic Flute* by Wolfgang Amadeus Mozart, Austria's best known Freemason, which is supposed to include many Masonic symbols.

The room is entered from the west end through two massive bronze doors sculpted with scenes of the building of Solomon's Temple. Each one weighs one and a quarter tons and moves on five hinges at the gentlest of touches. Inside there is space for twenty-eight London buses, or, more practically, 1,700 seated people. The room is 123ft (37m) long and 62ft (19m) high, and its focus, as in a church, is on the east end where, on the ceiling cornice, Solomon and Hiram stand on either side of Jacob's ladder heading towards heaven. The whole ceiling frieze is made of millions of mosaic stones that pick out the figures of Prudence, Temperance, Fortitude and Justice as well as the all-seeing eye of God as the Great Architect of the Universe, and the Ancient Greek mathematicians Euclid and Pythagoras. On the floor in the centre of the hall a black-and-white chequered carpet, patterned in the manner of a Masonic 'pavement' on which, in some lodges, members are required to walk 'on the square'. This means taking steps forward and backwards or sideways, but not diagonally.

Freemasons have many rules and regulations. One of the rules is that members cannot discuss either religion or politics. They are not a Christian organisation, but they are monotheist. Members in the United Kingdom must believe in a supreme being, any supreme building. Atheists cannot join, although they can in France, while in Scandinavia they must be Christian. The Catholic Church has been consistently against Freemasonry, even considering it a cause for excommunication, while the Church of England fuddles along. When Dr Rowan Williams, the Archbishop of Canterbury, appointed a known senior mason, Rev Jonathan Baker, as Bishop of Ebbsfleet in 2011, he was backtracking on a previous pronouncement that Freemasonry was incompatible with Christianity.

The degree of secrecy, mysticism and ritual practices of the Craft have led Freemasons to be compared with the Roman cult of Mithras, whose worshippers called themselves *syndexioi*, or hand-shakers. In fact, as their symbols of set-square, level and plumb-line imply, they seem to have grown out of the fraternity of masons that travelled around Europe in the Middle Ages picking up work in cathedrals, castles and any other large building that required their skills. Because they were itinerant, they could not belong to any city livery company, such as the Worshipful Company of Masons, which forbade their members taking their skills abroad. Their fraternity also lacked the parishes and patron saints to which all London guilds or mysteries were attached. They therefore began to meet in taverns where they formed lodges and, perhaps wanting conversations that involved a little more than talk about the shaping of stones, they admitted into their fraternity others who shared similar beliefs. What they lacked in tradition, they began to make up for in elaborate ritual.

A Grand Lodge came together at a tavern called the Goose and Gridiron in St Paul's Churchyard in 1646, some thirty years before Sir Christopher Wren's cathedral gave masons full employment. Other taverns were chosen by other lodges, and in 1775, when there were more than 400 lodges in England, the Grand Lodge opened its own **Freemasons' Tavern** at 61 Great Queen Street. The property was a five-bay mansion with another building behind, which the Lodge occupied to establish the first purpose-built Masonic hall. This could be hired by non-Masonic organisations, such as the Anti-Slavery Society, which started life here. The building on the street meanwhile was leased to a landlord as the Freemasons' Tavern.

A rival, Antients Grand Lodge, was set up a little over a hundred years later, and when the two lodges finally buried the hatchet, or maul, in 1813 and came together as the United Grand Lodge of England, Sir John Soane, architect of the Bank of England, was appointed the Masons' Grand Superintendant of Works for the task of expanding the building. This contribution was all but obliterated in the 1860s when the architect Frederick Cockerell built the second Hall.

The Freemasons' Tavern continued to prosper, but it was much more than a pub. The food writer Lt-Col Newnham-Davis described its appearance and function in 1899:

"The Tavern is not what the name implies. It is a restaurant with a public dining room, with a fine ballroom, and with many private dining-rooms. Its outside is imposing. Two houses stand side by side. One is of red brick with windows set in stone, and is Elizabethan in appearance. The other, of grey stone, is of a style of architecture which might be called 'Masonic'. From the pillars of the second storey there rises an arch on which are carved the figures of the zodiac. In front of this are stone statues representing four of the Masonic virtues, of

which Silence, with her finger on her lips, is the most easily identified."

The figure of Silence can still be seen to the right of the balustrade above two Corinthian pillars on the remaining frontage of the Freemasons' Tavern, while on ground-floor level a plaque commemorates a dinner held in the tavern in 1807 to inaugurate the world's first geological society.

In the first decade of the 20th century the Tavern was transformed into the **Grand Connaught Rooms**. Refurbished and expanded in Edwardian grandeur, they included a great hall that seated 800. Their name comes from the Freemasons' most effective Grand Master, the Duke of Connaught, who had been in office eight years at the time of their renovation in 1909. Continuing the Tavern's hospitality, the Connaught Rooms have always been a sociable place, with more than two dozen halls and rooms that can be hired for parties, functions and meetings. Today they are leased to a company that organises venues, and in 2013, the Football Association returned to celebrate the 150th anniversary of their founding in the Freemasons' Tavern.

Since its inception, the UGLE's Grand Master has been a member of the royal family, though never, by their own regulations, a monarch. Prince Arthur, Duke of Connaught and Strathearn, was Queen Victoria's favourite third son and seventh of nine children. Too far down the line to expect the crown, he was packed off to join the army, and spent time in South Africa and India, where he represented the royal family in the 1903 Delhi Durbar. But mostly he was in Canada, where, in 1911, he was appointed Governor-General.

The Duke of Connaught's lasting contribution

to the fabric of London was the Freemasons' Hall, built as a memorial to the 3,225 masons who had died at the Front during the First World War. The Masonic Million Memorial Fund, his campaign to raise the necessary million pounds from masons, was over-subscribed, and an international competition, chaired by RIBA's president Sir Edwin Lutyens, chose the plans of H.V. Ashley and Winton Newman to build a new hall. For this, the last of the 17th-century houses in Great Queen Street and Drury Lane were bought and demolished, creating a two-and-a-half acre open space that allowed the Art Deco façade to be fully appreciated when approached from Long Acre.

The building opened in 1933 as The Masonic Peace Memorial, but peace did not last. At the outbreak of the Second World War in 1939, it was renamed the Freemasons' Hall. That same year the Duke of Connaught relinquished his post, and his nephew, Prince George, Duke of Kent, tied his Grand Master's apron strings.

The Duke of Kent died in the war when his son was only seven, and it wasn't until 1967 that Prince Edward, Duke of Kent and a cousin of the Queen, was elected Grand Master. He is the last of the royal Grand Masters. When Prince Andrew, second in line to the throne, was approached to succeed him, his grandmother disapproved.

"Have nothing to do with the Freemasons," Queen Elizabeth the Queen Mother is reported to have said. "Leave it to the Kents."

Whatever the reason for the royal disfavour, the secrecy surrounding Freemasons and their practices has always aroused suspicion, leading to their banishment in many countries. There is no better evidence of their underground nature than the 'discovery' in 1990 of a magnificent Masonic Temple hidden behind a false wall in the basement of the **Great Eastern Hotel**, now called Andaz Liverpool Street, at Liverpool Street station.

The hotel had been built at the same time as the station, which was the terminus for trains arriving from the Continent via Harwich, and until the late 20th century it was the only hotel in the City of London. It opened in 1887, and in 1912 the Freemasons took over two rooms in the hotel to furnish in their own no-expense-spared design to use as meeting rooms. On the first floor they created an Egyptian-inspired hall, and in the basement they devised a Greek temple, a sumptuous hideaway of marble pillars, mahogany and gold that is now listed.

The installation of a temple inside a hotel was not unusual at this time, and they could be found in several of the more luxurious establishments, such as the Cecil Hotel in the Strand, where in 1898 immigrant Italians formed Loggia Italia, Britain's first Italian-speaking lodge, which is still in existence, or the Savoy, where from 1909 the American Lodge met. Six years later one of the most spectacular modern Classical temple buildings opened in Washington, DC. **The House of the Temple**, based on the Mausoleum of Halicarnassus and designed for Freemasons practising the Scottish rite, was the work of John Russell Pope, architect of the Jefferson Memorial, who had been the first prize-winner at the new American School of Architecture in Rome.

In London, Freemasons' temples were also built into the larger restaurants, and there was even one in the Theatre Royal in Drury Lane, established in 1886. Lord Kitchener was a member of the Drury

Lane Lodge. But to the outside world, the discovery of the Greek temple during renovations of the Liverpool Street Hotel by the Conran Group in 1990 came as something of a surprise: the hotel had fallen into a state of disrepair, the Freemasons had departed and the sellers had not known it was there. What the incoming hoteliers uncovered was a room with a throne beneath the all-seeing eye of God, and the motto *Aude, Vide, Tace*: Listen, See, Be silent. There is a marble pavement, the room is lit by Art Deco wall lights, and rays from a golden sunburst on the ceiling point to the signs of the zodiac.

Built under the direction of the Duke of Connaught, who occupied its throne at its opening, the temple is now hired out for corporate dining, fashion shoots and other glamorous events, and as a result has become too expensive for the Freemasons, who returned occasionally during the 1990s, although it is still sometimes used by overseas lodges. The Egyptian Temple, meantime, was lost before it could be listed, and has been turned into a gym.

Today, Freemasonry is a much more open organisation, emphasising its friendliness and charitable works. Freemasons' Hall, its museum and library were opened to the public in 1985 and there are regular tours. The United Grand Lodge of England has a quarter of a million members, and worldwide there are reckoned to be six million. Each country or region has its own Grand Lodge and they are independent of each other. There is no overarching figure or organisation.

A mason visiting London might also include a look at another temple, in **Mark Masons Hall** just over a mile away at 66 St James's Street near St James's Palace. This is the home of The Grand

Lodge of Mark Master Masons of England and Wales and its District and Lodges Overseas. Its Grand Master is the Duke of Kent's younger brother, Prince Michael of Kent, and it acts as the administrative centre for seven separate Masonic orders: Mark Masons, Royal Ark Mariners, Order of the Secret Monitor, Royal and Select Masters, Order of the Allied Masonic Degrees, Red Cross of Constantine, and the Knights Templar. The building, a former club house, has five floors with a temple on the ground floor, and among its treasures is a lump of limestone from King Solomon's quarries.

The restaurant, with a view of St James's Palace, is open to the general public for lunch.

LOST BASTIONS OF TRADE

Most of the institutions on which London has prospered are visible in some shape or form today. However, two that played key roles in its development, and in the establishment of the whole culture of Britain, have left little or no trace. The first is the **Hanseatic League**, the second the **Honourable East India Company**.

In the early Middle Ages London lacked a proper mercantile structure for importing goods, and the community that was just beginning to re-establish itself after centuries of Viking raids relied on foreign cargoes arriving on ships from Germany, Flanders and France to trade on the Thames waterfront. In time, German merchants from the Guildae Aula Tutonicorum formed the Hanseatic League, an early Common Market initiated by Lübeck for the herring trade, which established links around the Baltic Sea in Russia, Scandinavia, Poland and across the North Sea. It would eventually involve some 170 cities. In London, German trade was granted privileges in a decree of Henry II in 1157, commanding the relevant authorities to offer the merchants of Cologne protection of "*all their wares, and merchandise and possessions, so that you injure neither them nor their house in London, nor their merchandise, nor impede their business, nor permit any of these things to be done.*"

The 'house in London' of the Cologne merchants was to become the Hansa **Steelyard**, the largest trading complex in Britain. For 600 years the self-governing enclave dominated the waterfront above London Bridge where Cannon Street station is today, remembered in Steelyard Passage, which forms a link beneath the station along the Thames Path. Built to defend itself against local hostility as well as any threat that might come up the Thames, it had high, fortified, mostly windowless walls with three gates and a double-headed eagle over the main entrance in Thames Street, locked at nine o'clock every night.

The enclave was self-sufficient and if necessary could have stood a long siege. Vines grew in a fruit and vegetable garden, and there were a number of living quarters, halls, warehouses, kitchens, plus an inn, chapel and guildhall, with masters and men drawn from any of the many Hanseatic towns. Hansa merchants would set out their wares, and each new shipment brought London buyers in search of goods. In terms of trade at the time, this was a major market place, bringing a cornucopia of items from all over the known world, places most Londoners would never visit and could only dream and talk about. Men of the moment, ever anxious to have their fingers on the pulse of events, would regularly visit the Steelyard's wine house in a corner of the recreational garden, which dispensed Rhenish wine from its copious cellars.

The Steelyard took its name from the *Stalhof*, a

weighing device that stood by the wharf where cargo was unloaded and loaded. Imports were mainly wine, wheat, timber and tar; exports were woollen cloth, beer and hides. Its administrative centre was a large stone Guildhall, sometimes called the Easterlings Hall to differentiate it from the City's Guildhall, and an alderman was elected from their number to represent them in the City. The merchants were required to bear arms and were pledged to help defend their host city if necessary. One of the duties of the Hansa merchants had been to keep Bishopsgate in good repair. From here the road out of London led north to the Norfolk port of King's Lynn, where a brick warehouse standing on the quayside is the sole remaining piece of evidence that England was ever part of the great Hanseatic League.

Hans Holbein the Younger arrived at the Steelyard on his second stay in England in 1531, painting portraits of the merchants to use as samplers, which he hoped would find favour with Henry VIII. He also decorated their Guildhall with two large murals, *The Triumph of Poverty* and *The Triumph of Riches*, which have not survived, though preparatory drawings are held by the Bodleian and the Louvre.

There were no women or families in the Steelyard. Merchants who undertook tours of duty were unmarried, remaining for a period of between three and five years under a *Stalhofmeister*, master of the Steelyard, obeying the strict rules of the Hansa, which gave the place a monastic air. There was a chapel in the grounds, but Sunday worship mainly took place in nearby **All Hallows the Great**, which the merchants generously endowed with stained glass, stalls and an oak screen carved by craftsmen from Hamburg.

All Hallows burned down in the Great Fire of

1666, as did the Steelyard, which was rebuilt, but by then it had lost much of its power to growing world trade, while the Hansa cities of Europe began to be absorbed into the political entity of nations. For a short time it was closed by Elizabeth I, who wanted her piratical admirals free from competition, but it remained the property of the free towns of Lübeck, Hamburg and Bremen until 1853, when it was sold to private speculators.

As the power of the League shrank, a new force was founded that would affect nearly every aspect of British life: its language, its culture, its food and its population. Given a royal charter in 1600, the Honourable East India Company was one of the most successful joint-stock companies the world has seen. Backed by its own private army that would number 200,000, and given a monopoly in Britain on all trade east of the Cape of Good Hope, it became an agent of the government until the company was dissolved and the Indian subcontinent became a part of the British Empire following the Indian Mutiny of 1858.

East India House, the company's headquarters, was one of the most celebrated buildings in the city. Standing at the corner of Lime Street now occupied by the Lloyd's Building, its spectacular 200ft (60m) neoclassical frontage was known as 'the Monster of Leadenhall Street'. It grew out of the mansion of Sir William Craven, elected Lord Mayor in 1610, and it was extended by degree, reaching its final state in 1798 with the designs of the Company surveyor, Richard Jupp, and Henry Holland, architect of Carlton House, who would follow him into the post. Above a central portico with six Ionic fluted columns, Britannia sat beside a lion with the world at her feet; Asia was sitting on a camel; Europe rode a horse.

Inside, court rooms, sale rooms and committee meeting rooms had much gilding and many mirrors, maritime motifs, statues of Company men and pictures from the stations around the East. Its valuable library had "every book published on the subject of Asia" as well as a fine collection of Chinese and Indian manuscripts. Among its literary clerks was Charles Lamb, the essayist and author of the popular children's book, *Tales from Shakespeare,* published in 1807. Born to a barrister father in Inner Temple, Lamb toiled in the accounts department for twenty-five years, explaining, "My printed works were my recreations. My real works may be found on the shelves in Leadenhall Street, filling some hundred folios."

The public knew the building best for its museum of souvenirs amassed by employees through centuries of travel to the East. Free to the public on Saturdays, it covered three floors, and was a treasure trove of unusual objects, though most were without labels, so visitors had to try to guess their provenance. It would be their first glimpse of the art, crafts and religion of Buddhists, Sikhs, Hindus and Taoists who would one day build their temples in London.

In the basement were models of buildings and small figures, boats and carriages, agricultural implements, paintings of potentates, all kinds of musical instruments, and a great variety of textiles. On the first floor was a regal throne in silver and gold, miniature paintings, ivory carving, stone statues, arms and decorated cabinets, with glass cases of jewels and examples of women's costumes. The top floor showed all the natural products of the East. But what most people wanted to see was Tipu's Tiger, a wooden automaton of a life-size tiger savaging an East India Company soldier. Turning a handle caused the tiger to roar and the man's hand to rise as he wailed in pain. It had been made for the amusement of Tipu Sultan of Mysore, and was seized when the Company took his palace in 1799. It is now in the **Victoria and Albert Museum**, where much of the East India House collection was taken. Some items reached the **National Maritime Museum**, where they have been displayed in a long-running exhibition, while nine miles of shelving at the **British Library** were installed to take the Company's letters, ledgers and books.

The Company's business spread through the neighbouring streets, and up to 4,000 were employed in its warehouses, which were rented as and when they were needed. Permanent storage was established in 1768 when more than five acres of land was purchased in New Street, on the north aside of East India House. The first buildings begun by Jupp were the **Bengal Warehouse** and **Tapestry Building** in New Street, off Broadgate. These were followed by a complex of six-storey blocks that by 1820 covered the site with a main entrance on Cutler Street, after which they were named.

Following the Company's demise, the warehouses were taken over by St Katherine Docks before being subsumed into the Port of London Authority. The **Cutler Street Warehouses** were the last major storehouses in the City, and they were finally abandoned in the 1970s when the ports lost out to containerisation. Bought by Standard Life and Greycoat Developments in 1978, they were partially demolished, in spite of a campaign to save this virtually untouched Georgian enclave hidden behind massive, fortress-like brick boundary walls. Architectural salvage firms had a field day, especially with such prize items as 18th-century glass and iron windows. The buildings that remained were scrubbed up for white-collar use by Seifert's architectural firm, with added elegance for the entrances and railings by Quinlan Terry. Stone stairs, iron columns and brickwork were thoroughly cleaned to reinforce the blocks' magisterial air.

The estate was further developed with a mix of refurbishment and new six-storey blocks in 2006 when it adopted the more aristocratic name of the adjacent **Devonshire Square** to describe the whole area. A glass canopy was added to keep the weather out of the West Courtyard, a square of original buildings, and shops and residential apartments were designed to make a 'campus environment', a secure place to live and work. The community atmosphere is now emphasised through such activties as a local choir, and the main gates are closed at 10pm every night.

Estate agents appointed to sell apartments have relied heavily on the warehouses' history in their sales pitch, aiming particularly at potential buyers in Asia and invoking the Poet Laureate John Masefield and the lines he wrote describing the cornucopia of cargoes after a visit in 1914. In fact, Asian buyers may know more about the most magnificent surviving warehouse complex in the City of London than Londoners, who may come here for an Indian meal at the Cinnamon Kitchen or a cocktail and oysters in The Old Bengal Warehouse but see little sign of its past. While it is true that both St Katherine Docks and the Port of London occupied the buildings more than twice as long as the East India Company, both benefitting from trade beyond the East, it is the Company that built these wonderful warehouses and establshed London as the centre of world trade. Only outside Devonshire Square is the name of East India House evoked, given to a block on the north side facing Middlesex Street re-styled in 1982.

Better known as Petticoat Lane, Middlesex Street was once one of the East End's most notorious markets. It owed its existence in part to the fact that it was right beside the warehouses and handy for the disposal of goods stolen from Cutler Street. Much could also go missing between the warehouses and Blackwall in Poplar, where the Company had been building its East Indiamen, the largest vessels in Britain's merchant fleet, since 1614. On arrival, ships anchored in the Thames and lighters took their high-value goods to the 'legal quays' in the Pool of London, where they would be landed and inspected before being transported to Cutler Street to be sold.

The Company buildings, including almshouses set up in 1627, spread around Poplar, and in 1803 the **East India Docks** for importing and exporting cargoes were added to their fiefdom. Covering some thirty acres, they were the world's biggest private naval facility, handling up to 250 vessels at a time in what was the closest that East Indiamen could sail to the city. Wartime bombing, slum clearance and dock closures have left little trace of the docks and the Company's dominance of East London. The docks are now reduced to a nature pond, though an impressive stretch of the 20ft- (6m)-high perimeter brick wall remains in Naval Row, enclosing glass office blocks, water features and streets with spice names. The Company coat of arms with two 'sealions', literally lions with fish tails, can be seen in the pediment of **Meridian House** in Poplar High Street, which was built in 1801 under Henry Holland for the Company's chaplain. Nearby is the **East India Chapel**, the oldest building in Docklands, dating from 1667 and since renovated and renamed St Matthias. Its ceiling boss has the original coat of arms, depicting three ships. These are small relics from such a global giant.

Despite the absence of any sign of the Company in both Poplar and Devonshire Square, others are happy to cash in on the East India Company name. A shop in Mayfair's Conduit Street, for example, uses it to market 'fine foods' that are 'quintessentially British flavours with a touch of the Exotic'. In fact, the British palate has acquired such a liking for the East Indiamen's 'Exotic' cargoes that there are now said to be more Indian restaurants in London than in Mumbai and Delhi put together.

A final taste of the Company can be had in the **East India Arms**, a red-brick corner pub built against Lloyd's Register of Shipping in Fenchurch Street. In a single room there is standing-room only for the suited insurance men who gather beside a smattering of pictures of ships and Eastern ports. Open only on weekdays, it belongs to the Kent brewers Shepherd Neame, who produce an IPA, an Indian Pale Ale, the sugar- and hop-heavy brews designed to travel east for the men of the Honourable Company and their successors, the thirsty colonials of the British Raj.

AN EMPIRE'S GLORY

One of London's best addresses is **Ten Trinity Square**. At the end of 2014 its doors open not just to guests in a new 120-room luxury hotel, but also to residents in thirty-seven serviced apartments on the top four floors, the choicest of which have views across the **Tower of London** to **Tower Bridge**. It is not the five-star service or the panorama that make this a special place, however. It is the building itself. **The Port of London Authority headquarters** was designed as a temple and beacon to the merchants, seamen and dock workers who made Britain rich, and despite its multi-million pound makeover, it remains a shrine to an empire.

Described variously as 'in the Beaux-Arts style' and 'Edwardian Baroque', the monumental, ethereally-white building expresses the enormous power and dignity of the river. The layout is a perfect square facing the four cardinal points with its southeast corner knocked off to front Trinity Square Gardens. Here Corinthian columns are three storeys tall, and all the main decoration of the building is at the same height as their flamboyant capitals. The fine lines of the Portland stone cast intense shadows as it rises through styles that hint at distant parts of the world, from Greek Mausoleum to American Art Deco. At its height, in an ornamental tower thirty metres tall, is a scrubbed Father Thames, Poseidon–like, with a triton in one hand, the other pointing down river towards the sea. Around him allegorical figures populate projecting pavilions: a winged Prowess standing in a galleon drawn by sea horses represents Exploration; Agriculture, torch raised, drives a chariot and team of oxen led by the figure of Husbandry; Commerce has a basket of goods and produce; and bold, bare-breasted Navigation stands on a globe, one hand on a ship's wheel, the other on a sundial. The Scottish sculptor Albert Hodge died before his designs could be made, but from his sketch models his assistant, Charles L.J. Doman, completed the task.

The building's central secret was the Rotunda, a courtyard covered by a reinforced concrete dome the size of the dome of St Paul's, protruding no further than the height of the surrounding inner walls. Like the old Reading Room at the British Museum, it had concentric circles of desks, counters used by clerks, and from this interior the four wings were accessed through porticos, each with a medallion portrait of a naval hero: Cook, Drake, Hawkins and Nelson. Inside, the largest of the many wood-panelled rooms was the boardroom, with a portrait of Geoffrey Chaucer at one end, and at the other a coquettish Samuel Pepys wears a broad-brimmed, be-ribboned hat and a wig of curling locks that seem to have been bought by the pound.

"*The room interiors are perfectly delightful with their medieval wealth of detail in the carving,*" wrote Arthur Mee in 1936. "*It is as if an army of craftsmen had lived here for years out of the world's storms, quietly carving symbols of the ships that brave the storms, and the merchandise that they bring from the ends of the earth."*

In spite of the industry of the river, once so packed with vessels that it was possible to walk across them from one bank to the other without getting wet, the governing Port of London Authority was not set up until 1908. Until then, the docks had been in private hands, competing with each other and offering various terms and conditions. The PLA would bring order to the chaos of the world's greatest port and manage the seventy miles of tidal water from Teddington to the Nore lighthouse in the estuary.

The location for this new landmark was not difficult to decide upon. Tower Hill was already concerned with mercantile trade and the sea. The elegant headquarters of **Trinity House**, the organisation that oversees navigation on rivers and coastal waters, had been here for more than a century, though when Pepys was its Master it was still based in Deptford. Pepys was also Clerk of the Acts of the Navy Board, which had both offices and accommodation on the west side of Trinity House, in Seething Lane. Samuel and Elizabeth lived there, and they are buried in their church of St Olave's on the corner of what would become, in the PLA scheme, Pepys Street.

The Navy Board buildings were on ground that until the Reformation had been occupied by the Friars of the Holy Cross, or Crutched Friars. After the Navy Board moved out it became a warehouse owned by the London and India Dock Company, and known as the Crutched Friars Warehouse. This warehouse provided 1.5 acres for the PLA site, which was doubled by the acquisition of surrounding buildings that were demolished, with another street planned on the new building's south side. This was Muscovy Street, a name inspired by The Czar's Head, a pub in Great Tower Street where Peter the Great used to drink when he came to London to learn shipbuilding in Deptford, borrowing boats from the Navy Board to practise his seamanship on the Thames.

Below this nautical hill lay the whole Pool of London, with the Tower of London, Customs House (nine Corinthian columns) and Old Billingsgate Fish Market along its banks. Halfway up the hill is **All Hallows by the Tower**, one of London's oldest churches. With Roman pavements in its crypt and a Saxon arch, it was saved from the Great Fire by Admiral William Penn, father of the founder of Pennsylvania, who ordered naval personnel to destroy buildings around the church to create a fire break, while Pepys climbed the spire to watch the conflagration. Nautical relics inside the church include a crucifix from the Spanish Armada, the crow's-nest barrel from Shackleton's *Quest* and model ships left as votive offerings.

The south side of Tower Hill has always been a largely open space, created for William the Conqueror's **White Tower** in the 11th century when a royal enclave an arrow's-shot wide was kept clear for defensive purposes. The hill was subsequently used as a place of execution, but in the 1790s, a decade or so after the last scaffold had been dismantled, the garden was laid out as a formal, fenced-off oval for the residences of what was becoming a smart square. Setting the style was Trinity House, a perfect neoclassical building with engaged Ionic columns on the upper floor, designed by the organisation's surveyor, Samuel Wyatt, who was responsible for both the building and the gardens.

In 1909 the PLA put their new building out for

competition, which was won by Yorkshire-born Edwin Cooper, an enthusiast of the Corinthian order, who would be knighted for this work. But by the time construction began on the Trinity Square site, the First World War had broken out and it was not completed until 1922. By then, there was another monument to be erected on Tower Hill. The simple but moving **Tower Hill Memorial** in the shape of an open-ended Greek temple 70ft-(21m)-long commemorated the 12,000 seamen of the Merchant Navy and the Fishing Fleet who had lost their lives during the war. Many had died as a result of mines laid in the North Sea, and from U-boat action in the Atlantic.

The Memorial has a circular disc at the centre of its roof, like a squashed funnel, and it has been described as "an idiosyncratic marriage between a Classical temple and a modern ship". Its architect, Edwin Lutyens, had no appetite for the war, but he knew about life at sea. He spent many months in the more peaceful waters of the Mediterranean and the Indian Ocean, travelling half a dozen times to oversee the building of the Viceroy's four-and-a-half-acre 'House' in Delhi. That was where he headed for when war broke out. He also took a liner to South Africa where he had produced a study for the University of Cape Town. On a return trip he befriended the captain and idled his time away by designing for him a perfect captain's house. Later that same year, 1917, he visited northern France with the fledgling War Graves Commission, and as a result designed the **Cenotaph** in Whitehall as well as around 150 war memorials at home and abroad. In these cemeteries men and officers were laid side by side, "irrespective of creed or class". In particular,

Lutyens wanted no sign of the crucifixion or "the inherent cruelty of the cross".

But there were no graves for the seamen. Bronze plaques covering the walls bear the names of vessels and the crew who died at sea. These were designed by the Glaswegian sculptor William Reid Dick, who had seen service in France in the Royal Army Medical Corp, which he had joined on the outbreak of war.

"War," Luteyns declared in despair, "is anathema to architecture."

In the Second World War, during which the architect died in his bed, war was more than an anathema to architecture. It was a ruthless destroyer. Aerial bombing cost the City and the docks the best of its buildings, and the Port of London Authority Headquarters, Trinity House, and All Hallows by the Tower were all badly damaged. Great treasures were lost and restoration took time.

Nearly six years of conflict also cost another 26,933 seamen's lives and they deserved a memorial, too. Trinity Gardens was acquired in perpetuity by Act of Parliament for the War Graves Commission, and a sunken garden and memorial wall behind Lutyens' temple was designed by the Commission's chief architect, Edward Maufe. A plaque was also set in the ground to mark the Tower of London's execution spot.

There was no money or labour to fully restore the PLA Building, but what remained provided sufficient meeting space and kudos to attract the new United Nations, which met here among London's ruins in 1946 to sign its first charter. The Authority returned to the building, which it used until the 1970s when it followed the docks downriver to the Royal Terrace Pier at Gravesend where it remains. The building never fully recovered. The Rotunda was not replaced, and a nine-storey block was plonked in the courtyard, but it never really worked. For a time the building was occupied by London insurance brokers Willis, until they moved to Foster's **Willis Building** opposite Lloyd's in 2008.

Money from Asia has given the PLA Building a new lease of life. KOP Properties of Singapore and China's Reignwood Group are the new owners. Architects Woods Bagot worked with English Heritage to get the best out of the existing building. The recently inserted nine-storey office block was removed and a glass canopy roof installed with a central well, dubbed The Whirlpool. Behind the building, after archaeologists finished rooting around Bronze Age remains, Seething Lane Gardens have been re-laid, and Pepys is back on his plinth.

THE EXCHANGES

The most imposing Classical temple in the City is the **Royal Exchange**. Once the centre of London trading, it was a great bazaar that rang with the shouts of buyers and sellers, of arguments, hard bargaining and done deals. All manner of goods were bartered in a Babel of languages. Whole shipments of sugar, coca, cotton, timber and other raw materials were invested in and gambled on. Goods were retailed in the upper galleries, spices were stored in its vaults by the East India Company, Lloyd's insured shippers against risks, and the quadrangle echoed to the clamour of dealers on the stock exchange until their behaviour and bad language caused them to be expelled.

"*There is no place in town,*" Joseph Addison wrote in the *Spectator* in 1711, "*which I so much love to frequent as the Royal Exchange. It gives me a secret satisfaction, and in some measures gratifies my vanity, as I am an Englishman, to see so rich an assembly of countrymen and foreigners consulting together upon the private business of mankind, and making this metropolis a kind of emporium for the whole earth.*"

The hall no longer echoes to the sound of money being made. No shouting comes from the salesmen in Bulgari, Tiffany, Louis Vuitton, Gucci, Mont Blanc, Hermés, or any of the other luxury outlets in the building, and voices are muted over champagne and seafood platters in the Royal Exchange Grand Café that occupies the central square.

Images from the history of Britain's commercial life can still be seen, however, in the Mezzanine where the Grand Café has further tables. Even when there is a notice to say that the Mezzanine is closed, visitors can go up the stairs and ask to see these large murals from a walkway that runs all the way round the building. Not great art, the paintings are nevertheless a curiosity, illustrating incidents from the past, from the first Phoenician traders in Cornwall, by Lord Leighton, to the fire that destroyed the previous building and women workers in the First World War. The story ends with a painting of King George V and Queen Mary visiting the First World War battlefields of France, and on the steps of St Paul's, by which time the Exchange's use was waning.

This temple to commerce is a reminder of London's status as a world capital of trade. The first building on the site was established through the efforts of Thomas Gresham, a wealthy city merchant with a bank and a street named after him. He is credited as starting the banking system in England, and his Exchange, inspired by visits to the *bourse* in Antwerp, had an open courtyard and more than a hundred shops on its upper floors. Much of the building material for the first Exchange came from the Low Countries, too. It burnt down in the Great Fire of London, and its replacement suffered the same fate. That one had a covered piazza surrounded by 'walks', which were named after their destinations or nationalities, such as Virginia, Jamaica, East India, Jews, Spanish, Muscovy. This, too, burned down, in 1834. The third and current building was by William Tite and it was completed in 1844. Two blocks were cleared around its entrance to add a statue of the Duke of Wellington to the imposing portal. In this surfeit of space, a trio of Classical buildings that includes **Mansion House** and the **Bank of England** created the City's heart and soul, its Temple Mount on Cornhill.

Temple-style in Portland stone, the Royal Exchange has reassuringly sturdy Corinthian columns supporting a triumphant pediment containing the heroes of Mammon: a figure of Commerce gripping the Exchange's charter, surrounded by the Lord Mayor and by London and overseas merchants. Along the architrave are words from Psalm xxiv 1: "*The Earth is the Lord's and the fullness thereof.*" The names of both Elizabeth I, who opened the first exchange in 1571, and Queen Victoria, who did the honours in 1844, are written in gold, and tradition insists that on these steps any new monarch of the United Kingdom is announced.

Grey marble, known as Turkey stone, on they floor of the large central quadrangle is from the original Exchange. Around it, three storeys with pillars and balustrades rise to a glass dome, and offices occupy the upper floors. Like religious houses, the Royal Exchange faces west, and at its east end a clock tower, a campanile with a peel of thirteen bells, competes with surrounding church steeples. The original bell summoned merchants at noon and 6pm, and a subsequent arrangement of bells played regional folk songs. Just before they crashed through the roof of the Exchange in the fire of 1834, they were reportedly playing *There's nae Luck aboot the Hoose*. On top of the bell tower is a gold weather vane in the shape of a grasshopper, the adopted symbol of the Greshams. A statue of Sir Thomas in hose and doublet poses jauntily at its base.

Before Sir Thomas came along, trading was carried on in coffee houses, each business favouring a particular place, and these continued to act as centres for information, mail and gossip. Increasingly popular, by the mid-eighteenth century there were around one hundred and fifty, many of them close to the Exchange where dealers in particular markets would gather at their favourites, such as Jonathan's in adjacent Change Alley where stock brokers met. But as the city grew, there was also a need for purpose-built exchanges to handle domestic products such as corn and coal, so vital for the burgeoning London population.

The **Corn Exchange** started out in 1745 in Mark Lane, which runs parallel to Seething Street just west of the Port of London Authority building. This tumultuous street of warehouses and offices was one of the busiest parts of the City. Its Greek Doric architecture arrived in 1828 with a colonnade and a covered, domed roof. A lively feature in the journal *The Leisure Hour* of 1856 describes the scene on market day:

"*It has just struck two on a Monday afternoon, as we mount the steps from the lane, and, elbowing our way through the entrance, begin to look around. The whole market, roomy as it is, is so crowded with dealers, factors, and speculators, that we have no other choice but to go in any direction that chance may leave open. There is a confused unceasing babble of sounds, for five hundred people are talking at once; but a decent and commendable decorum prevail; and though jokes and laughter are not wanting, those vulgar demonstrations which are too often their accompaniments in similar places are not observable. The frequenters of the market comprise a variety of classes, among which we notice the unmistakable face, keen yet stolid, of the city speculator, the bluff country gentleman, the Kent farmer, and a sort of semi-nautical specimen, who, we are informed, is the privileged hoy-man or his descendant, who, by virtue of an ancient prescriptive right, which his ancestors earned by supplying the city of London with food in a time of plague and famine, has certain market-dues remitted to him and his representatives for ever. Then there are the factors who supply the bakers with meal and flour, and there are the bakers themselves, a round number of whom generally find their way to Mark Lane on a Monday, to furnish themselves with the number of sacks of flour it is their fortune and their function to 'do' in the course of the week. But these are not all. Ere proceeding far, we are brought up by a group of Greek faces, and the soft musical sounds of their, to us, unintelligible tongue; an energetic, fiery- eyed, and dark-skinned group it is, yet tamed, it is plain, by the phlegm of our northern example, to the outward suppression of their oriental eagerness and vivacity. Further on, the guttural consonants of the German greet us with their long familiar sound; and shortly after, a hand is laid upon our shoulder, belonging to none other than our old acquaintance, Monsieur Germani, whose business it is to watch the phases of the market on behalf of a well-known French firm..."*

Damaged in the war, the Corn Exchange reopened in 1954 and was reconstructed in 1973, but in 1987 it moved into the **Baltic Exchange** in St Mary Axe where it continued its Monday market sessions. The

Baltic Exchange started life in the Maryland Coffee House in Threadneedle Street, changing its name in 1744 to the Virginia and Baltick Coffee House. This was where merchants and master mariners trading in the American colonies and the Baltic Sea met to hear news and check for mail. It was, and still is, primarily a mercantile and shipping exchange, concerned with the world's freight chartering. Progressing through a number of premises in the area, its finest headquarters were built in 1903 in Jeffrye Square, now St Mary Axe. Its pediment, which bore Britannia with a lion, and shipping scenes, was supported by granite columns. Grey marble was the feature of the great domed trading floor, which Arthur Mee, writing in the 1930s, described as "the holy of holies of the commercial magnates of the City".

Left severely shaken by the IRA bomb in Bishopsgate in 1992, the Grade II listed Baltic Exchange building was, against much opposition, pulled down. Stained-glass windows that survived, commemorating the fallen of two world wars, were sent to the **National Maritime Museum** in Greenwich where they are enshrined in a special display. The mountain of beautiful stone and plasterwork went through several dealers, at one time appearing on the website of an architectural salvage firm that suggested that it might suit a millionaire interested in jigsaw puzzles. Eventually, the job lot was bought by an Estonian businessman for £800,000 and shipped in forty-nine containers to Tallinn where it is hoped one day it will be restored. The site of the exchange, at No. 30 St Mary Axe, was sold off, allowing Foster + Partners to build the **Gherkin**, and the Baltic Exchange's business continues in the building next door at No 38, where Balls Brothers has a restaurant and bar.

Questions were asked about the necessity of demolishing such a fine building, but there had been a much bigger fight thirty years earlier to prevent the demolition of the **Coal Exchange** in Thames Street. This landmark building was on a corner site, which allowed the portico entrance to be shown to great effect, curving through ninety degrees beneath a circular tower. The main attraction was its pioneering cast-iron rotunda, rising through three galleries, which was extensively and exquisitely decorated with figures of miners, colliers, and the tools of their trade, as well as botanical and geological elements, such as fossils and trees, from which coal is formed. A wind dial was installed to help predict the arrival time of the cargoes.

The Coal Exchange was designed by the City of London's architect, J.B. Bunning, and during its construction a Roman bathhouse was revealed, though it was not properly excavated until the road widening of the 1960s. Prince Albert, arriving in a royal procession by boat, declared the Coal Exchange open in 1849, and no doubt found some ideas for his forthcoming glass and cast-iron Great Exhibition in Hyde Park. It was the last day in October and fires were burning across the city, creating the usual smoke and smog. Coal was as vital to London as corn. A tax on it had funded the rebuilding of the City after the Great Fire of London, and by the time the Coal Exchange opened around 12,000 shiploads of coal from the North-East were arriving each year, employing 20,000 seamen: it was a collier from Whitby in Yorkshire that brought Captain James Cook to London, and another, the *Prospect*, berthed in Wapping, that gave London one of its most famous pub names.

The Coal Exchange suffered some bomb damage during the Second World War but it was the nationalisation of the industry that meant it would never open for business again, and the building was converted into offices. It remained a landmark, and though its condition in its latter years deteriorated, the chairman of the Streets Committee, who wanted it demolished to widen Thames Street, overstated his case at a hearing in 1962. He described it as "dingy and devoid of beauty", and as for its admired ironwork, he had "seen better in boarding houses in Ramsgate and Hastings".

This was at the end of a four-year battle to save the building, in which the Victorian Society negotiated the removal of the rotunda to Australia's National Gallery of Victoria in Melbourne, a city known for its Victorian architecture. But it never happened, and the building was pulled down.

One exchange that has survived is the **Hop Exchange** by Borough Market on the south bank of the Thames, which made it convenient for the hop fields of Kent and the brewers of Southwark. Built in 1866, its architect was R.H. Moore. A long, curving frontage sweeps down the road from London Bridge, and a fine wrought-iron entrance gate is topped with a tympanum of rustic figures of a hop picker, farm labourer and porters. Cast-iron columns bring elegance, and colour is provided in the Great Hall by a red and black patterned floor and by red shields emblazoned with the white horse of Kent on attractive iron balconies, painted green. It is now given over mainly to offices, but the Great Hall can be hired for events.

THE EXCHANGES

The only exchange in Europe retaining an open-outcry trading pit is the **London Metal Exchange** in Leadenhall Street, the world's largest metals marketplace with warehouses around the globe. It started life in a coffee shop where a ring would be drawn in the sawdust and traders would gather round to barter. Today the Ring is a red-leather circular seat, where members sit for each of the consecutive five-minute slots that are devoted to particular metals. Some, like cobalt, may not produce much response, but copper can have them on their feet, gesturing furiously. Behind them, clerks act as intermediaries between the floor and the dealers, who operate in booths, phones clamped to their ears. It is pure theatre.

A shout away from the Royal Exchange was the **Stock Exchange**, which stopped being a public spectacle in 1990 when the IRA left a bomb in the viewing platform of the twenty-six storey block in Threadneedle Street. But by then deregulation and the Big Bang meant trading was no longer face-to-face and not so much fun to watch. The Brutalist concrete tower, built in 1972, was also starting to look dated among the flashy glass towers rising all around. At first Nicholas Grimshaw was asked to glaze its exterior and extend it, but then the building was abandoned altogether, and the Stock Exchange took a leap not into the world of steel and glass, but into a sober arrangement of modern Classicism, relocating to Paternoster Square by **St Paul's Cathedral**. The millennium was approaching. Conservationists and Prince Charles were concerned. There was a need for something more enduring than glass. It was time to revert to Portland stone.

This area on the north side of the Cathedral,

once a centre of publishing and still home of the **Worshipful Company of Stationers and Newspaper Makers**, had been hurriedly and unhappily redeveloped after being flattened by wartime bombing. After much debate, a master plan was drawn up by the William Whitfield partnership that had to incorporate Wren's surviving red-brick Chapter House. The centerpiece of the square is homage to Wren and his associate Robert Hooke, in the form of a stone column with a golden flame on top, a Monument in miniature, which acts as an air vent. In 2004 the Stock Exchange moved into a building on the north side of the square where unadorned columns and a portico are a modern take on a vaulted colonnade. Goldman Sachs and Merrill Lynch moved in, too.

The Mitsubishi Estate Company of Japan bought this once public corner of London for development. Now signs warn: *"Paternoster Square is private land. Any general licence to the public to cross this land is revoked forthwith…"* That is why activists in the Occupy movement, who attempted to camp outside the Stock Exchange in 2011, were kept at its gates. Or, specifically, its famous gate, **Temple Bar**, the former western gate to the City at Westminster's boundary, designed in Corinthian style by Wren with Stuart monarchs in Roman garb and sited in Fleet Street. Its connections with the financial world are not new. Behind leaded windows, the upper rooms, which can be hired, were once rented by Childs the bankers to store their accounts. In *Old and New London* (1874), Walter Thornbury wrote: *"There is preserved here, among the costlier treasures of Mammon, the private account book of Charles II."*

Recovered at the cost of a token £1 after more

than a hundred years in exile in the Hertfordshire estate of Sir Henry Meux, a wealthy brewer, Temple Bar was restored to act as an appropriate new entrance to the emporia of Mammon. But it has been installed back-to-front. The huge wooden gates can be locked and bolted only on the St Paul's side. So instead of keeping the mob out, the mob could, theoretically, lock the money-makers in.

TEMPLES OF SHOPPING

For more than a century London's two temples of shopping have been **Harrods** and **Selfridges**, the largest and second largest stores in the country. Not only do thousands pass through their doors every day, but they are seldom long out of the news. Mohamed Al-Fayed, for twenty-five years the owner of Harrods, might not always have wished to see reports about him and his store, which he ran with idiosyncratic enthusiasm, declaring, "This is not Marks and Spencer or Sainsbury's. It's a special place. There is only one Mecca." Selfridges, on the other hand, has spawned a TV series, first broadcast in 2011, with Jeremy Piven playing its equally idiosyncratic, headline-making owner, the American Harry Gordon Selfridge.

The story of modern consumerism starts with the Great Exhibition of 1851, an occasion for London's entrepreneurs to drum up ways to make money from the impending hordes heading for Hyde Park. Twenty-five years earlier Charles Henry Harrod had opened a draper's and haberdasher's in Borough High Street before becoming a grocer in Stepney. When he saw the opportunities that the Great

Exhibition might bring, he purchased the current site in Old Brompton Road. It was a smart move and he prospered. A fire burnt the store down in 1883 when in the hands of his son, another Charles Harrod, and the current building rose from the scorched five-acre site. It is a hotch-potch of styles – Beaux Arts meets Queen Anne – held together by the warm richness of terracotta tiles. A walk around the block shows pedimented dormers, bay windows, Romanesque arches and, at the rear in Basil Street, four-storey Egyptian columns.

The main architect of the building, completed in 1905, was Charles Stephens, after whom Harrods' 2013 Christmas teddy bear was named, dressed in a pinstripe waistcoat and red tie. Bears have been a feature in the store since 1921 when A.A. Milne stopped by to purchase a bear for his one-year-old son, Christopher Robin.

Christmas is a good time for Harrods, when more than quarter of a million customers come shopping each day. The façade is spectacularly illuminated for the season, but the outline of its dome and upper floors is also distinctively lit during the rest of the year with around 12,000 bulbs describing its shape.

Inside, the most glorious part of this vast temple of consumerism is the Food Hall, or halls, with sculpted tiles by Barnsley-born William James Neatby, who was to become the chief artist at Royal Doulton in Lambeth. These are particularly evident on the raised ceiling of the Meat and Fish Hall beneath which caviar and roasts are served to diners perched on stools on marble pedestals. There are around thirty restaurants in the building as well as 330 departments, served by some 5,000 staff from 50 different countries. Statistics lie thick on the ground of the store that promises *Omnia, Omnibus Ubique* – All things for all people everywhere.

But it is in the **Egyptian Hall** that Al-Fayed, the Pharaoh of Harrods, has left his mark. In this central well, escalators connect the six floors, rising beside huge pillars, lanterns, lotus leaves, bronze balconies, sphinxes and carved panels in a fantasy journey up the Nile to a ceiling of stars and signs of the Zodiac. This is the imaginative work of William Mitchell. Born in Maida Vale in 1925, Mitchell worked for the London County Council in the 1950s and '60s, and designed panels for the Liverpool Metropolitan Cathedral before becoming Al-Fayed's artistic advisor. Two sphynxes facing each other on the lower floor of the Egyptian Hall turn out to be busts of Mitchell and Al-Fayed, who became honorary chairman of the store after he sold it to Qatar Holdings for a reported £1.5 billion in 2010. The sculptor has his metal sculpting knife between his claws, and with an inscrutable smile Pharaoh Al-Fayed grips a model of Harrods store.

The sphynxes sit on plinths at the entrance to what might be described as Harrods' crypt. Here candles burn at a shrine to Al-Fayed's son, Dodi, and Diana, Princess of Wales, their colour portraits side by side before a small pyramid where a glass container holds the diamond-studded engagement ring Dodi supposedly bought for the princess in Paris the day before the car crash in which they died. In front of this altar, Mitchell's larger-than-life bronze sculpture of the pair beneath an albatross is inscribed 'Innocent Victims'. A book of condolences is open nearby.

Mitchell is in no doubt about his creative achievement in the Egyptian Hall. He says, "This is the one project, which without hesitation, or embarrassment, I feel I am able to call my masterpiece."

Harry Gordon Selfridge, once dubbed "the Earl of Oxford Street" has no such legacy. Even the personalising apostrophe was dropped from the store's name after he was ousted from it half a dozen years before his death, though his book, *The Romance of Commerce*, a history of trade from the time of the Phoenicians, is back in print.

Like Harrods, Selfridges hit its stride in the Edwardian era when shopping began to be more than a chore for the middle classes. Selfridge was pivotal in this transformation, creating a store in which women, in particular, could feel at home. A millionaire with a common touch and a showman's flair, Selfridge made shopping an event, putting Blériot's plane on display just after it had made the first Channel flight, and inviting John Logie Baird to make his first public demonstration of a television.

After the stock market crash of 1927, and following years of high spending, Selfridge died almost as poor as he had been born. Ambition had driven him up the ladder at Chicago's Marshall Field, a major store today owned by Macy's, and taken him up the aisle with a property heiress. By the time he arrived in England to build his Oxford Street store, he was rich. For the London project he chose one of America's best-known architects, Daniel Burnham, who had been Director of Works for the great Columbia Exposition in Chicago that celebrated the 400th anniversary of Columbus landing in America. Burnham also designed New York's Flatiron and started the whole Beaux-Arts style that defined the Chicago School. He had never studied art or architecture, but sharing the fruits of his success, he offered to pay for young Frank Lloyd Wright to go to Paris to study at the École des Beaux Arts. The fledgling Modernist had other ideas about his – and architecture's – future and turned the offer down, even though Burnham had just built what has been described as Chicago's, and America's, first skyscraper, the twenty-one storey Masonic Temple Building.

Burnham and Selfridge would have liked a taller edifice in London, but as it was they had to convince the authorities that their new-fangled steel-framed construction would stand up at all. They settled on five storeys, and in doing so helped to revise the city's building regulations.

Fluted, decorated stone columns disguise the steel frame on the outside of Burnham's building, which was initially just nine bays long, and it was not extended to include the main entrance and a further nine bays to the west until 1931. This was when it was given its *pièce de resistance*, the Art Deco *Queen of Time* sculpture by Gilbert Bayes that included a clock. Above the entrance canopy the 11ft- (3.4m)-tall winged figure stands on the prow of a ship with mermaids each side, cast in bronze with blue and green enamelling and gilding. There is also some stoneware from the Royal Doulton headquarters in Lambeth where Bayes had made an external frieze, now in the room at the Victoria and Albert Museum that is named after him. The Gillett & Johnston clock has four bells to strike the 'Westminster quarters', and a three-ton bell visible above the clock to strike the hour.

The fluted columns are repeated inside, and between the pair by the entrance is Edouard Paolozzi's large bronze statue of Josephine Baker.

Paolozzi's friend, the store's then managing director, Vittorio Radice, explained his decision to make the exotic dancer an icon in this once staid, middle-class store: "Gordon Selfridge and Josephine Baker were both Americans," he told the *Independent*. "They both did something revolutionary in the same era: one opened Selfridges and the other opened the Folies Bergère. And both died in poverty."

Frank Lowy, founder of the **Westfield Group** of more than 100 shopping malls worldwide, and the most successful modern builder of retail outlets, is unlikely to die in poverty. Born in Slovakia in 1930, the son of a travelling salesman, he grew up in Budapest. Just after the Nazi invasion of Hungary, when he was thirteen, his father left home to buy a ticket at the station and never returned. It was not until fifty years later that he discovered his father had been taken to Auschwitz where he was beaten to death for refusing to give up his prayer book. After fighting in the first Arab-Israeli war, Lowy went to Australia where, aged twenty-three, he started in business.

Westfield arrived in London in 2008 when it opened its Westfield London in White City, a mall of 255 stores, with further expansion due to be completed in 2017. Three years later **Westfield Stratford City**, Europe's largest mall, opened as part of the Olympic development. Its glass-vaulted, three-decked, crescent-shaped avenues provided the entrance to the 2012 Games. Sited on disused railway yards, and incorporated into a new transport hub, it put down a retail marker in East London in the same way that Canary Wharf did for finance houses. With all the big chains taking part, from Marks and Spencer to John Lewis, and with nearly three dozen food outlets, a cinema and casino, it seemed like a glittering island in a sea of dross.

The archaeologist Neil Faulkner, the author of *A Visitor's Guide to the Ancient Olympics*, compared the Hellenic Games with London's. He pointed out that half the original festival was given over to religious rites in honour of Zeus, father of all the gods, whose massive statue stood in a dazzling temple beside the Games. London's 2012 equivalent, he wrote, was Westfield Stratford City. This 'Temple of Capital', as he called it, was built in one of the most deprived urban areas in Britain, and locals could only 'gawp' at the high-priced designer stores, just as the ancient Greeks stood open-mouthed at the gold and ivory statue of Zeus.

CLASSICAL RAILWAYS

Fading framed photographs and newspaper cuttings in **The Doric Arch**, a popular Fuller's pub on the east side of Euston Square Gardens, tell the story of **Euston Arch**, the monolithic entrance that once heralded the world's first intercity railway. Erected in 1837, it remained an astonishing and somewhat anachronistic sight on Euston Road until the station's redevelopment in 1961, when it was demolished. Many people today would like to see the arch put back again.

Euston Arch was colossal by any standards. It was 70ft 6in (22m) tall with square pillars at each corner and four Doric columns 8ft 6in (3m) in diameter. On each side were two Classical pavilions with bronze gates to control the flow of passengers and traffic. It was built of Yorkshire gritstone and, having spent most of its life amid the smoke and grime of steam locomotives, it was a dismal grey.

Robert Stephenson's London and Birmingham Railway Company employed Philip Hardwick as its architect. Born in London, Philip was the third generation of distinguished Hardwick architects, and his inspiration for the Euston Arch, and its twin at the other end of the line in Curzon Street in Birmingham, which is still standing, came from a tour of Rome. His design was not strictly an arch at all, but a *propylaea*, a monumental gate based on the 5th-century BC entrance to the Acropolis in Athens.

Its arrival in London added to a homage to ancient Greece that had been established across the road in **St Pancras New Church**. The giant plane trees growing along its length seem a deliberate attempt to hide from public view the most unashamed Classical religious building in London. Deisgned to look just like a temple, it has no south entrance, as one would find on an English church, and the only entrance is through the giant wooden west-end doors beneath a portico of half a dozen Ionic columns. The steeple is modelled on Athens' Tower of the Winds and the roof is edged with palmate tiles, while the pillars around the interior apse are copies from a temple to Minerva.

Most pagan of all are the porches on each side of the building based on the Erechtheion, the temple on the Acropolis named after the Archaic king, Erechtheus. Both of these are supported by four caryatids, female figures made in Coade stone and constructed around cast-iron pillars that bear the weight of the roofs. The story is that when the sculptor, Charles Fossi, arrived to install them, he found that he had made them too tall, and so he cut a slice out of their midriffs on the spot. As they are cast in sections, it is hard to tell if this is true. The figures are holding water jars and inverted torches, their flames extinguished in a gesture symbolising death, since they stand at the entrances to the labyrinthine crypt designed to take 2,000 coffins and now used as a gallery space for occasional exhibitions.

St Pancras New Church was designed and built by the local architect William Inwood a dozen or so years before the Euston Arch appeared. He would have seen one of the original Acropolis caryatids that Lord Elgin had recently acquired for the British Museum, where it can still be seen, and on receiving the contract for the church, he set off for Athens to complete his designs.

The church's foundation, laid by the Duke of York, is inscribed with a Greek translation: *May the light of the blessed Gospel forever illuminate the dark temples of the Heathen.* To some, it was a mystery why this inscription, which Inwood had taken from a temple that had been converted to a Christian church, should be written here in Greek at all. Many thought that the whole building was a step too far along the road away from Christian beliefs, and it hastened the revival of Gothic.

A paradigm of this high Victorian style can once again be found on Euston Road, and once again it is the product of the railways. George Gilbert Scott's Gothic Revival **Midland Grand Hotel**, five minutes' walk east of St Pancras New Church, is an integral part of **St Pancras**, one of London's most agreeable railway termini.

"*Railway stations and their hotels are the equivalent of cathedrals and monasteries,*" reported *The Builder* not long after the Midland Grand opened.

The railway's architect was the engineer William Henry Barlow, a Woolwich man whose grand tour was six years spent in Istanbul building manufactories for a British machine-tool maker. Not for him the glory of Greece or Rome. The station he built for the Midland

Railway in 1863 included the unprecedented cast-iron canopy spanning 240ft (73m), which remains, after major redevelopments, as impressive to the jaded modern traveller as it must have been to the Victorians when it first appeared.

The complex restoration of the station that began at the end of the 20th century prepared it to become the capital's premier terminus for Eurostar, the Olympics and for high speed trains from Germany and Spain, stealing the march on termini south of the river that once were the points of departure for the Channel ports and the Continent.

Unusually, the platforms at St Pancras were built on the first floor as the railway lines had to pass over the Regent's Canal immediately to the north. For the renovation, these were extended with a glassed-in area to accommodate the much longer Eurostar trains. Beneath the platforms is a vast undercroft, supported by cast-iron pillars brought from a defunct cotton mill in the Midlands. With easy access for vehicles, this had been used for storage and workshops. Today it is an up-market mall, with no place for low-brow outlets, and the majority of people attracted to the station are not passengers, but shoppers and diners.

Not a nail can be hammered into the Grade I listed fabric, so the station's whole new interior is free standing. It could be demolished tomorrow without harming one brick or stone. The spotlessly cleaned bricks, limestone, sandstone, granite and slate were brought here from English counties served by the Midland Railway Company. The iron ribs of Barlow's glass roof, transported from Derbyshire, have been painted in their original 'Barlow Blue', and English Heritage insisted that the intervening twenty-two coats of paint remained beneath, so the layers of history were not lost. A portion of the floor has had to be removed to give access between the two levels, which meant that a number of pillars from the undercroft had to be removed. These were taken to create an iron henge in the garden of Fawley Hill, the Buckinghamshire home of the railway enthusiast Sir William McAlpine, which holds steam and vintage weekends. Witty signs were put up to explain that this was the site of ancient worship of St Pancras, the 4th-century Roman martyr.

Scott's adjoining Midland Grand Hotel can be reached through the first floor Booking Office, now a bar and restaurant. The hotel takes its form from the medieval cloth halls of the Low Countries and some of its style from Lombardy Gothic, with warm brick and stone. The medieval flavour was enhanced by some two dozen stone masons who carved the different groups of figures at the base of each window's dividing pillar.

The Midland Railway Company was in fierce competition with its older rival and neighbour **King's Cross**, owned by the Great Northern Railway, a company more interested in freight than passengers. The Midland Railway therefore built its hotel to attract not just its own customers but also its competitor's. Coal transportation was Midland Railway's principal trade, and each guest room of the Midland Grand Hotel was furnished with an open fireplace. Larger rooms on the first floor had pianos, too. Despite its enticing exterior and glorious interior, the hotel was not a great success. The rooms overlooking Euston Road were noisy, there was no running water and no en-suites, though chamberpots were of the finest Worcesterware. By the time the hotel was completed, it was already facing competition from more modern establishments closer to the excitements of the city. Aware that the open fires were a potetial hazard, the builders installed floor plates with 22in (5.5cm) of concrete, so plumbing, when it came, was difficult to instal. Closed in 1935, the hotel was used as railway offices and renamed St Pancras Chambers. Neglect followed, and instead of being restored, many decorations and frescoes were simply painted over.

By the 1960s both Euston and St Pancras were in need of rescue. The decision to pull down Euston Arch was met with enormous opposition, but it went through anyway, despite the fact that, as the *Architectural Review* remarked, it was *"one of the outstanding architectural creations of the early nineteenth century and the most significant – and visually satisfying – monument to the railway age which Britain pioneered."*

Leading the fight to retain Euston Arch were the poet John Betjeman and the architectural historian Nikolaus Pevsner. When they failed, they started the Victorian Society and they were soon at work again, campaigning to save the Midland Grand Hotel from the demolition men. It might have suffered the same fate, but the outcry that had been caused by the destruction of the Euston Arch acted as a break, and the building was saved.

Interest in the Euston Arch was reawakened in 1993 by the architectural historian Dan Cruikshank with a television programme about its fate. This revealed that the demolition contractor, Frank Valori, who was thought to have numbered the stones and sent them off to storage, had in fact furnished his garden at Paradise Villas in Bromley with choice chunks. It was subsequently discovered that about

60 percent of the material, some 40,000 tons, had been used to level the bed of the Lee River's Prescott Channel at Three Mills in Bow.

The programme sparked new interest in the Arch. A trust formed by Cruikshank to campaign for its reinstatement continues to this day. Its patrons are Sir William McAlpine and North Londoner Michael Palin. The pub on the corner of Euston station, meanwhile, changed its name from The Head of Steam to The Doric Arch, and there were hopes that HS2, the high-speed rail to Birmingham, when and if it came, would find a place for the arch in its schemes.

In 2005, plans were drawn up for a £150 million five-year refurbishment to rescue the Midland Grand Hotel, which is owned, like the station, by a consortium of British and Continental railways. Rooms that the hotel's staff once occupied beneath the slate roof were turned into apartments by the Manhattan Lofts Corporation, and the fascinating flat in the Clock Tower, with grand views, has been made available by its occupier for short rents. The rest of the building was brought back to life as the five-star **St Pancras Renaissance Hotel**, leased to the Marriott chain. It has thirty-eight period suites in the main part of the building and a £3,000-a-night Sir George Gilbert Scott suite. Most guests, however, are given one of 207 rooms in the new Barlow House wing, named after the station architect, that stretches alongside the British Library and Francis Crick Institute, matching as far as possible the original.

Like many great pieces of architecture, Gilbert Scott's Midland Grand Hotel fell short of its ambitions, even though the original plan he submitted was for a far larger hotel than the competition rules had demanded. The Gothic façade of this 'monastery' has a number of niches for statues that remain empty. What figures would be most appropriate to put in them today might be a question to put to budding artists in the University of the Arts that occupies the **Granary Building** on the north side of the station in the vast King's Cross development, one of the last surviving industrial buildings in London from the steam railway age.

LONDON TRANSPORT

Stockwell and Acton are not places that immediately come to mind when contemplating the great buildings and institutions of London. But bus and tube enthusiasts will instantly recognise these highspots of their devotion.

Stockwell Bus Garage, opened in 1952, was chosen by the writer Will Self for a talk he gave at the Royal Academy of Arts in 2011, titled 'London's Most Important Building'. The garage was, he declared, *"architecture as vaulting ambition"* and *"Modernism at its best"*.

The architects, Adie, Button & Partners, worked with engineers A. E. Beer to overcome the post-war steel shortage by producing an unprecedented concrete dome. The architect George Mountford Adie was a leading Modernist in thrall to Le Corbusier and Frank Lloyd Wright. Most notable of the private commissions he undertook was **Charters** in Sunningdale, Berkshire, in 1938, described a few years later in *Country Life* as *"The last great country house to be built in Britain"*. Winston Churchill was a visitor and it was used as a bolt-hole by the Duke and Duchess of Windsor. The Art Deco buildings are now elegant apartments.

Rather different, then, is his bus garage, though

4: INDUSTRY

Adie did spend the war years designing army barracks. His philosophical and spiritual side was fed by the teaching of George Gurdjieff, the guru of 'esoteric Christianity' who died in 1949, and his later life was spent in Australia continuing to teach Gurdjieff's method of 'consciousness awakening'. Imagination was certainly required to create 74,422 sq ft (6,914 sq m) of space with no iron or steel and no obstructive pillars. Ten overarching hinged ribs are spaced between skylights that illuminate the area, which is enough to accommodate 200 buses serving thirteen routes.

The overall effect when seen from afar, said Self, was of "*a series of monumental whales' backs, as if a pod of these leviathans has been frozen in mid motion as they coursed through the choppy brick seas of inner London suburbia*". The writer had lived nearby since 1996, and he viewed the garage and its multi-ethnic staff as embodying the changing population of the increasingly cosmopolitan city. "*Seeing the herd of double-deckers queuing for admission, I'm driven to think of the vast distances they've traversed that day, linking the entirety of London together, then finally returning to their spiritual home, this temple of transportation.*"

As for Acton, the Underground's former workshops are now the **London Transport Museum Depot**. Among nearly half a million items are signals, signage, maps, carriages, clocks, station furniture, old buses, early American-inspired 'cars', aluminium trains killed off by graffiti artists and prototypes that never made it. There are some 80 vehicles, including horse-drawn buses and a working steam engine once used on the Underground. Researchers comb the archives and volunteers sit silently indexing train timetables and heaps of tickets.

There are photographs and engineering drawings, too. But perhaps its greatest treasure is the thousands of posters commissioned by London Transport. The tradition was established by Frank Pick, who was made Head of Publicity in 1908. It reached a peak in the 1920s and 30s when up to 40 posters were produced every year: Man Ray designed a poster in which the London Transport logo is echoed in an image of Saturn; artists of the Grosvenor School provided a familiar style; John Bratby and David Hockney brought bright colours.

Few original works are here, but it does not matter: the poster was the thing, the real graphic art, showing extraordinary variety and ingenuity. Reprints, still for sale, provide London Transport with a valuable income stream. The Museum Depot is only occasionally open to the public, but this may change, particularly if the London Transport Museum in Covent Garden realises its assets and decamps to West London.

The identity of London Underground established so brilliantly by Pick, with station architects such as Charles Holden and the typographer Edward Johnston, belongs firmly to the 20th century. This identity was ruptured with the opening of the **Jubilee Line Extension** in the last months of 1999 before millennium fireworks exploded.

The addition to the Underground network brought a whole new way of looking at tube stations, overturning so much of the accepted order. The diddy Docklands Light Railway had connected the city to Canary Wharf and east as far as Stratford, rattling uncertainly at first on roller-coaster tracks, but it wasn't until the Jubilee Line's massive stations opened the floodgates to commuters that London's

East End came out of the dark and into the steely glister of day.

Light was of the essence for the new tube stations. Glass, aluminium, cast iron and textured steel would bring skiesfull of it flooding into the great boxes that would be sunk in the cut-and-cover method that took stations to new depths. Between Green Park and Stratford there would be six entirely new stations and five enlarged or rebuilt. It needed a bold approach and a clear purpose, and Roland Paoletti was the man to oversee it. The commissioning architect's name was not one that crossed many commuters' lips, as he had spent much of his time out of the country. He had been born in the City to Italian immigrants, and he was sent to a Jesuit school in Curragh, acquiring the Irish burr that was evident for the rest of his life. He trained in Manchester, and moved on to Italy where he worked with the master architect-engineer Pier Luigi Nervi. Like Norman Foster a decade later, he gained his international reputation in Hong Kong, when he was appointed to develop the new Mass Transit Authority, which was to become one of the world's most profitable rail networks.

His idea for London was to give each station to a different architect, so that no one style would emerge. However, the contemporary materials and techniques that they used gave form and shape to their designs: brushed and satin steel for the bold pillars and struts, contrasting Brutalist concrete and, where they were able, lots of glass to let in light. Platforms were all a little different, but not much, with variations on metal and ceramic tiles. Some seats are no more than metal misericords, and Paoletti likened the tile work at **North Greenwich** to Istanbul's great church, Haghia Sofia.

"For the price of an underground ticket," he said, "you will see some of the greatest contributions to engineering and architecture worldwide."

The stations were no minor undertakings. Michael Hopkins' **Westminster**, which was already served by the district and circle lines, plunged to record depths as the 'station box' was excavated down to 1,128ft (39m). Giant in scale and breathtakingly bold, its huge stainless steel pillars and buttresses were matched in bravura by rough concrete walls. Giant overhead lamps compensate for the lack of natural light, filling the escalator well that is part *Metropolis*, part Escher, while darker minds have compared it with Piranesi's visionary *Carceri d'invenzione*, imaginary drawings of hellish prisons. Natural light is precluded by Hopkins' **Portcullis House**, built on top of the station as part of the development. This provides offices for one-third of the Members of Parliament and its strange chimneys, which are air vents, are meant to reflect the Gothic style of the Houses of Parliament opposite.

New stations were able to draw in natural light through acres of glass. The architect of **Canada Water**, Ron Herron, who died four years before it opened, had a reputation for the avant-garde since he proposed his 'Walking Cities' in the 1960s, in which mobile buildings would roam the world. Though his structure above ground is drum-shaped, it is no homage to the circular Arnos Grove and Southgate stations designed by Charles Holden and opened nearly seventy years earlier. When Paoletti took up his post, people kept asking him how he was going to deal with the legacy of Holden and Pick.

"I went out to look at one of those Holden stations once," he told the *Independent*. "I don't remember the name of it now. And I really couldn't see the point. To me it's all just a lot of stripped-down Classicism: little buildings with friezes and cornices and what have you. It's simply the British form of Italian fascism, London Underground doing gently what other people were doing in a ferocious way. That's not what I'm about at all: I'm an engineer... I love the Victorians, St Pancras."

Paoletti's ideas are embodied in Norman Foster's contribution to the new line at **Canary Wharf Underground station**. Above ground, canopies at the east and west ends drink in light, swallowing it into the cavernous box dug out of an arm of the former West India Dock 78ft (24m) deep and 869ft (265m) long. Its roof supports a new park. In the concourse seven central, oval-shaped concrete-clad pillars rise to a vaulted ceiling that spreads out as gracefully as angels' wings above an iconostasis of ticket barriers.

"Everybody keeps saying that it's like a cathedral," Paoletti said on its completion. "They're wrong. It actually *is* a cathedral."

TEMPLES OF POWER: I

Open House weekend in 2013 offered the last chance to look around **Battersea Power Station** before it was redeveloped. The response was overwhelming. More than 40,000 people queued for up to four hours for a final farewell to this massive shell that has stood heroically by the Thames since its closure thirty years earlier. It was the biggest event in Open House's twenty-one-year history.

Like a magnificent temple from antiquity, Europe's largest brick-built building had by now lost its roof, some of its walls and all of its colour. Its fine Art Deco interior had been plundered, its marble tarnished, tile work collapsed, and brass machinery that once shone like the golden statue of Athene had been carted off. A thousand pigeons had made it their home. Little was left but the majesty of the building's proportions, its arcades of fluted pilasters open to the elements, its four chimneys like the remaining corner pillars of a temple to Zeus held up by the gods. For three decades it had stood in splendid isolation on a 39-acres site with a 1,300ft (400m) riverfront where the raised arms of two rusting cranes provided a watergate portico. Giles Gilbert Scott designed both Battersea and **Bankside** power stations in the brick-cathedral style he had employed on Liverpool Anglican Cathedral, and it was popular. In 1939, the year after the first half of Battersea Power Station was completed, it was voted second favourite modern building in London after John Lewis. The *Daily Herald* described it as "*the flaming altar of the modern temple of power*".

It was innovative, too, pioneering a gas washing technique to cut down sulphur emissions and breathing life and warmth into Pimlico on the opposite bank. Water was inhaled from the Thames, heated into steam to drive the turbines, and then exhaled over the river to Pimlico to provide 10,000 households with heat and light. This low-emission power source was set up following the Great Smog of 1952, which resulted in an estimated 4,000 fatalities, and it was the first large project to tackle air pollution. Distribution was by the **Pimlico District Heating Undertaking**, owned by Westminster City Council, and it was centred on a 135ft (41m)- tall tower. Still the UK's largest thermal store, since Battersea's closure it has set up its own power source of natural gas engines to bring low carbon heating to 3,256 homes, fifty commercial premises and three schools in the Pimlico area.

The silver tower can be visited on the September Open House weekend. The rewards for those prepared to tackle the ladders and stairs is a spectacular view right across Westminster, as well as a vision of the latest developments, not just in Battersea on the opposite shore but at Lots Road a mile and a half upstream in Chelsea.

Plans were announced for a £1billion scheme to redevelop **Lots Road Power Station** in the same week that people were having a last look round Battersea Power Station. Until 1990 it had powered the Underground, and neither of these brick leviathans could find anyone to put them to use as imaginatively as **Tate Modern** had done with Bankside. Since these three power stations closed down and London Electricity, a nationalised body, was sold off, the city has had no electric power plant.

Electricity coming from any power station has to go through substations, which are needed to reduce the voltage for domestic and commercial use. One of the earliest still in use is the **Duke Street Substation**, behind Bond Street Underground. It doesn't look much like an industrial building. At each end is a domed, Classical pavilion, with pillars and pediments on all four sides and heavily panelled double doors to give access to the hidden chamber. The only clue to its function is a graphic symbol of a silhouetted man being struck by a bolt of electricity, and the words DANGER OF DEATH.

Most of the structure is buried underground. Through the rows of wide-arched 'Diocletian' windows peeping over the pavements on the side street, it is possible to catch a glimpse of the vast machinery that spreads far beyond the footprint of the building. Bare bulbs illuminate white-tiled walls, and metal gangways and ladders disappear into the bowels of the earth. A science fiction film could be located here. The flat roof of the building, not much above eye level, is reached via steps either side of the kiosk. This is **Brown Hart Gardens**, a large paved area surrounded by balustrades with seating and potted plants, an unexpectedly quiet spot in the middle of the West End. After an overhaul in 2013 the glass-walled Garden Café opened behind one of the kiosks, which will undoubtedly bring more people to appreciate this industrial curiosity.

Before the arrival of the substation, there had been a communal garden here, laid out for the benefit of the surrounding blocks of flats. In 1903 it was leased from the Grosvenor Estate to the Westminster Electric Supply Corporation so they could build their substation. Despite opposition to their plans, which would deprive the locals of a green space, the scheme went ahead. Its architect, Charles Stanley Peach, tried to ensure that, though trees were cut down and grass dug up, there would still be a place for the community to take the air. Brown Hart Gardens is about the size of a tennis court, a scale that clearly suited Peach who designed Wimbledon's Centre Court.

TEMPLES OF POWER: II

Water is the source of life, and it is certainly the source of London's life. It has also been a source of death, and when the polluted river of the industrial city reached its nadir in the Great Stink of 1858, during which parliament had to abandon Westminster, drastic action had to be taken to remove sewage as far away from the city as possible.

Joseph Bazalgette, chief engineer of the Metropolitan Board of Works, undertook the task of sending the waste and storm water out of London. Central to his scheme were pump-houses that were needed to draw water through his riverside embankment tunnels to sites downriver where they could be dumped back in the river or processed in sewage farms.

For this, two extraordinarily ornate pumping stations were built: **Abbey Mills** by the River Lee on the north side of the Thames and **Crossness** in the Kentish marshes by Barking Reach. These temples to steam power housed engines three storeys high, with beams as big as the trunks of mature oaks that rocked to make cast-iron flywheels turn. When they were up and running, they seemed sweet as a baby's cradle. And it is possible to still see them working today. Crossness is the finest, a temple of ornamental cast iron and a Victorian jewel. Its aesthetics as well as its power were appreciated right from the start in April 1865, when around six hundred of the city's great and good caught trains to the Essex marshes for the inauguration ceremony, and the Prince of Wales, who arrived by boat, started the engines. Now beautifully restored, the highly decorated cast-iron interior is a visual feast of polychrome ironwork, its brass buffed on machinery that volunteers maintain. With 52-ton flywheels and 47-ton beams, the rotative beam engines are thought to be the largest in the world. They worked up until 1956, and through the enthusiasts' efforts they are working again.

An architect assisting Bazalgette was Charles Henry Driver, whose ability to make cast iron graceful can be seen in a number of South London stations, as well as Southend pier. He also designed Abbey Mills, an incongruous Victorian outpost between Three Mills Island and the Stratford Olympic site. It was built in 1868 on the site of a flour mill belonging to a Cistercian monastery, St Mary's Stratford Lanthorne, and it takes the shape of a Latin cross, with a central dome and octagonal lantern. The exterior is highly decorated with coloured brick, candytwist drainpipes, and pillars with floral capitals. Originally there were two freestanding chimneys, one each side, 210ft (64m) high, from which the smoke from the coal fires escaped. They heated water for the eight single cylinder engines that had beams 40ft (12m) long and flywheels 28ft (8.5m) in diameter. The chimneys were dismantled during the war, for fear that enemy action might cause them to topple onto the pump house, though they had not been in use since the steam engines had been removed and electric power had taken their place half a dozen years earlier. Although the engines have gone, the glorious Victorian interior of ornate cast iron remains. It has three standby electric pumps that can come to the aid of the water authorities in emergencies, and it maintains Thames Water's archives, which are open to researchers.

Bazalgette needed two other pumping stations for his scheme, one by Deptford Creek and, more picturesquely, one in Chelsea opposite Battersea Power Station. This is the **Western Pumping Station**, which has a square brick chimney with triple blind arches rising like a campanile beside the railway heading for Victoria. The smoke stack still acts as a ventilation shaft, and the flue has a ladder that climbs 271ft (83m) to the top. Built in an Italianate style with a copper shingle roof, the pumping station raised the level of the sewage pipes so that their contents could be passed across London to the east. From its inauguration in 1875 until 1977 it also supplied compressed water for the London Hydraulic Power Company, which operated thousands of outlets across the city, from lifts and cranes to theatre curtains. Its 150 miles of pipes have since been used for fibre optic cables. The four original beam engines were replaced in the 1930s, and Grosvenor Dock, where coal barges arrived, now makes a water feature amid luxury apartments.

Crossness has a handful of steam days each year when the leviathans are set in motion. But in west London, at **Kew Bridge Steam Museum**, working engines can be seen every weekend of the year. The largest in this extensive collection is an 1820 Boulton and Watt beam engine 40ft (12m) high and weighing

250 tons, which Charles Dickens described as a "monster". Indeed it is, but the cost of heating the boilers to get it going means that it only operates on occasions.

Kew has a large number of Cornish beam engines, as it was the Cornish tin mines that started the whole industrial revolution. It was for this industry that Thomas Newcomen built the first steam engines to pump water up from great depths, and it was there that Richard Trevithick had the first stab at a steam locomotive. James Watt, with his business partner Matthew Boulton at the Soho foundry in Birmingham, then developed the rotative steam engine that would convert the up-and-down pumping action of the piston into a revolutionary motion, allowing wheels, gears, spindles and lathes to spin for all eternity. Their steam engine, the company claimed, had what the whole world wanted: *power*.

Watt had a workshop in his home, and it has been preserved intact in the **Science Museum**. Cluttered with tools and models, it is a shrine to one of Britain's greatest industrial figures.

THE TEMPLE OF HEALTH

In 1780, the most expensive bed to be had in London was at the Temple of Health in the Royal Terrace of the **Adelphi**. Overlooking the Thames, this exotic establishment was part of the neoclassical development designed by Robert and John Adam, aided by their brothers James and William. It took its name from the Greek *adelphoi*, meaning brothers. Greek was in fashion. The Adelphi was completed at the moment when the British Museum had acquired a fabulous collection of Greek vases from Sir William Hamilton, British Ambassador in Naples, to form the basis of its Department of Antiquities.

The Adam siblings grew up in Edinburgh, where their father was a master mason. Robert's Classical knowledge came from a Grand Tour of Europe, begun at the age of twenty-five, studying under Piranesi in Rome and visiting the 4th-century AD palace of the Roman Emperor Diocletian at Split in modern Croatia. On his return in 1764 he published an account of the palace and joined his older brother James in London where he developed his own style of Classicism, giving emphasis to decorative detail in plasterwork, painted panels, fireplaces and furniture, and becoming George III's Architect of the King's Works.

Diocletian's Palace was, he said, an inspiration for his highly ambitious project that turned three acres of sloping mudflats by the Strand into one of the most desirable quarters in town. The prestigious development attracted great attention: painters and craft workers arrived from the Continent and labourers brought down from Scotland were encouraged in their work by the daily wailing of bagpipes. New streets were laid out, named after the brothers, and the rows of houses employed the word 'terrace' in Britain for the first time.

One of these houses, slightly grander than its neighbours, was incorporated into John Adam Street for the Royal Society for the Encouragement of the Arts, Manufacturing and Commerce, today simplified as the **Royal Society of Arts**, of which the brothers were members. According to the RSA, the brothers saw the Society *"taking the central role of a church within their urban composition, a modern temple to the arts and science"*.

The RSA later expanded to fill houses Nos 2, 4, 6, and 8 where exceptional original plasterwork and paintings can still be seen. In the 1980s the warehouse area three floors below ground was turned into The Vaults restaurant, open to the public and serving lunches on weekdays. There is also an opportunity to appreciate the RSA's original Great Room and its densely populated painting series titled *The progress of human knowledge and culture* by James Barry, during the Society's free lunchtime lectures. The paintings have been described by the enthusiastic critic Andrew Graham-Dixon as "Britain's late, great answer to the Sistine Chapel".

The warehouse area inhabited by The Vaults was part of the essential engineering feat of the Adelphi development, which raised and levelled the ground by three storeys to create an area at the same elevation as the Strand, to which the underground warehouses, lit with Diocletian windows and brick port holes, extended. This was the first time that the river had been embanked, and the idea was soon adopted at Somerset House, though both would be left high and dry when the Embankment cut them off from the river.

Above ground, where a large 1930s Art Deco block by Thomas Colcutt and Stanley Hemp now stands, was a square of twenty-four, four-storey quality homes, eleven facing north, one at each end, and eleven in the south-facing Royal or Adelphi Terrace with a promenade overlooking the river. The Adam brothers themselves took one of these next door to the actor David Garrick. The pastel-coloured ceiling from Garrick's drawing room is now on the ceiling of Room 118e in the British Galleries of the **Victoria and Albert Museum**. Decorated with scrolls, griffins and festoons with paintings of Apollo and the Four Seasons by the Italian Antonio Zucchi, it gives an idea of the splendour of these homes.

Half a dozen years after their completion, Dr James Graham, the world's first sex therapist, moved into the house the Adam brothers had occupied to create his exotic Temple of Health. The tall, handsome Scottish showman quack was on a mission to ensure procreation, lecturing on the subject of sexual health while his acolytes sung, recited and posed as figures from antiquity. The Classical fabric of the house was richly suited for the pleasures on hand for the price of the two-guinea entry. His own inspiration had been sparked by his encounter in America with Native Americans, whom he claimed had shown him cures unknown in Britain, and with Benjamin Franklin's electricity. He installed a number of devices for cures and well-being, including crowns, chairs and baths that tingled with the latest sensation.

The high point of this farrago was the 'magnetico-electric pathway to Elysian love-making' involving the Great Celestial State Bed, which couples could hire for fifty pounds a night. Twelve feet long and nine feet wide, this opulent vehicle where 'perfect babies could be created' stood beneath a heavenly blue canopy supported by forty glass pillars. The exotic atmosphere was plumped up with pillows and quilts and suffused with perfumes and music, while beneath the bed The Hauksbee Influence Machine, a glass sphere that crackled with primitive electricity, supplied the necessary celestial fire.

The fact that the bed was guaranteed to bless its incumbents with progeny was a powerful selling line to the aristocracy anxious to maintain its dynasties. Lady Spencer, whom he had met on the Continent among the high society of Spa, gave Graham money, though she became disillusioned when the machine failed to work for her daughter, Georgiana, Duchess Devonshire, despite the requisite douching in champagne and compliance with the recommended bodily contortions.

The Temple of Health was not used solely by those in search of procreation. It was in the address book of just about every rake in town, and there were lectures on diseases and wellbeing, at a guinea a time, and advice and pamphlets on diagnoses and cures. An Apollo chamber contained 'celestial ether', while crutches, ear trumpets and other accoutrements of the invalids that were no longer needed were left on show like votive offerings. An undoubted aid to visitors' general well-being was Hebe Vestina, 'the rosy goddess of youth and health' who talked on the nature of love and beauty throughout the progressive ages of life from her Electrical Throne in the Apollo Room.

One of the most popular of Dr Graham's goddesses was fifteen-year-old Emma Lyon, who here learned to perform her 'attitudes', evocative poses of mythological figures that would one day beguile Sir William Hamilton into marriage and Horatio Nelson into scandal and fatherhood. The daughter of a Cheshire blacksmith, Emma had what a later admirer, Lord Bristol, Bishop of Derry, would describe as a 'Dorick dialect', a reference to the country peasants of ancient Greece. But barefoot and in a flowing *chiton*, tossing her glorious chestnut hair, her innocent glances reflected in the many mirrors beneath the ceiling's mythological figures and Classical motifs, she was a peerless Hygeia, goddess of health, although sometimes, it was said by her many later detractors, she would romp naked in mud baths, treatment that the vegetarian Dr Graham believed could prolong patients' lives. Indeed, he may have invented the mudpack, and he used to give lectures while encased up to his neck in warm earth, convinced that in this way the body could absorb sufficient nutrients to sustain life.

For all his ingenuity, Dr Graham's success was short-lived. The Temple of Health moved briefly to Schomberg House in Pall Mall and lowered the price of its bed, but it lost money. Despite the generosity of former clients who rallied with financial support, closed in 1784, whereupon the doctor returned to Scotland, discovered religion and died of starvation aged forty-nine, shortly after publishing a pamphlet entitled *How to Live for Many Weeks or Months or Years Without Eating Anything Whatsoever.*

ATHENA'S MEN-ONLY CLUB

If an Englishman's home is his castle, then his club is his temple, an exclusive place of comforting ritual and spiritual refreshment where the like-minded can find solace in the knowledge that they are the chosen few. In London the most impressive clubs are not far from the royal court, in Pall Mall. Seen from Piccadilly Circus, their starting point is marked at the bottom of Lower Regent Street by the 138ft (42m) **Duke of York Column** with a figure of the soldier famous in a children's rhyme for pointlessly marching his ten thousand men up and down hill. In fact Frederick, younger brother of the Prince Regent, has been maligned, as he is credited with turning the British army into an efficient fighting force, outlawing such corrupt practices as the selling of commissions, and proving himself a competent commander-in-chief during the Napoleonic Wars.

His statue pin-points **Waterloo Place**, which was laid out to commemorate the battle of Waterloo that ended hostilities in 1815. On the east side of this square is the **Institute of Directors**, which until 1977 was the United Service Club. On the west side is the **Athenaeum**. These twin temples to male fellowship, facing a square of commemorative statues, are the focus of the street of hallowed clubs.

The United Service Club was the Duke of Wellington's personal favourite. It had been founded in 1815, the year of Waterloo, to provide a familiar, mess-room atmosphere for officers thrown out of commission and trying to find their feet on civvy street. At first, a club house was built half-way down Lower Regent Street, but it was plain and not much to their liking. At the bottom of the street at that time was **Carlton House**, a splendid mansion much more to their taste, which the Prince Regent had turned into one of the finest residences in Europe. Before leaving to do final battle with Napoleon at Waterloo, the Duke of Wellington had been honoured with a fête in the gardens where pavilions were specially designed by John Nash for the benefit of the 2,000 guests. Nash was at that time in the process of constructing the whole Regency highway that began at Henry Holland's Carlton House and led up Regent Street to Portland Place and Regent's Park.

Half a dozen years later, the battle won and George III dead, the Prince Regent was bounced down the road to Buckingham Palace as George IV. Suddenly a large central area had been vacated that would do very nicely for a Waterloo memorial. Carlton House was pulled down, but not without some recycling, notably the porticoes that were moved to provide side entrances to the new National Gallery. In its place was built Carlton House Terrace, fronting The Mall, and in its grounds the commemorative Waterloo Place was laid out between the two matching clubs on Pall Mall: one for officers, one for gentlemen.

The man behind the gentlemen's Athenaeum
was John Wilson Croker, a long-standing friend of
the Duke of Wellington and for many years Secretary
to the Admiralty, but not himself a military man.
With a dozen like-minded people, he created the
club in 1823 "for the Association of individuals
known for their literary or scientific attainments,
artists of eminence in any class of the Fine Arts,
and noblemen and gentlemen distinguished as
liberal patrons of Science, Literature and the Arts".
The number of members was limited to 1,200, no
more than nine new members could be elected each
year, and members would be excluded by "one
black ball in ten".

The plan initially had been to make the two clubs
a matching pair, but it didn't quite work out that
way. John Nash took on the United Service Club
while his protégé, Decimus Burton, aged just twenty-
four, designed the Athenaeum. For inspiration, they
looked to the pervading fashion for all things Greek.
Rome might have been all right for the Emperor
Napoleon, who wanted to create a new Rome in
Paris, but the British were going for the original, the
Hellenic, the real deal, especially now that Elgin's
marbles had just turned up in London.

In Ancient Greece an Athenaeum was a temple
dedicated to Athena, goddess of wisdom (Minerva to
the Romans) and used by teachers and scholars as a
place of learning. The most famous was the
Parthenon, the main temple on the Acropolis in
Athens, where the frieze had come from and where
the golden statue of Pallas Athena stood. Edward
Hodges Baily, who would go on to greater heights
with a figure of Admiral Nelson to top the Trafalgar
Square column, was chosen to create a suitable

Athena to stand above the Athenaeum's Doric columns and first-floor balustrades. For a model, he turned to the Athena Velletri, a statue named after the town in Italy near Rome where it was found, itself a copy of a lost Greek statue by the sculptor Kresilas from 5th-century BC Athens. Missing parts had been added, and the completed statue was part of Napoleon's plunder, ending up in the Louvre, where it can still be seen. Her Corinthian helmet made her a fitting choice, as this emphasised one of Athena's roles, as goddess of just wars.

It was only late in the day, with the unveiling of the Elgin marbles, that Croker decided the Athenaeum would not be complete without a copy of the Parthenon frieze on the front of the building. Croker was a man of great enthusiasms and persuasive arguments, and against some opposition he arranged for the Scottish sculptor John Henning to carry out the commission. Henning had seen the plundered pile of Greek marbles, and with Elgin's encouragement had gone back to early drawings of the Parthenon to work out the sequence of the stories told on the frieze, to put them in order and to fill in the gaps and so determine the way they would be displayed in the **British Museum**. The most important part of the story was the long procession of the Panathenia, a festival held every four years at which the goddess Athena was presented with a new *peplos*, or cloak. The scene would appear at the centre of the Athenaeum frieze immediately behind the golden statue.

Having established the narrative of the frieze, Henning had been making miniature model casts of it to sell in boxed sets. Now, at an enormous cost to the Athenaeum, he made a half-scale copy to run round three sides of the building. The money that was required for the project represented five percent of the entire building costs, and it was used at the expense of an ice-house, which many of the members would have much preferred, to ensure the refreshment of their syllabubs and lemonades. The episode led to a popular ditty:

I'm John Wilson Croker, I do as I please,
Instead of an Ice-House I give you a... Frieze!

The building was completed in 1829, and from the start the Athenaeum was the queen of clubs, a home-from-home for the best-known names in town. Its founders included the artist Thomas Lawrence, who provided a painting of George IV – his last act on earth was a brushstroke on the king's medals – and the sculptor Francis Chantrey, who immortalised Croker in marble. Sir Walter Scott contributed tomes to the outstanding library and Michael Faraday, the first secretary, installed electric light and died here in an iron-wheeled bath chair that is still on view.

The club aimed to provide all the comforts a gentleman might wish for, and its rule book strictly forbade gratuities to staff. In *The Curiosities of London* in 1867, the antiquary John Timbs described this male paradise:

"For thirty guineas entrance, and six guineas a-year, every member has the command of an excellent library (the best Club library in London) with maps; of newspapers English and foreign; the principal periodicals; writing materials, and attendance. The building is a sort of palace, and is kept with the same exactness and comfort as a private dwelling. Every member is a master, without any of the trouble of a master; he can come when he pleases, and stay away when he pleases, without anything going wrong; he has the command of regular servants,

without having to pay or manage them; he can have whatever meal or refreshment he wants, at all hours, and served up as in his own house. He orders just what he pleases, having no interest to think of but his own. In short, it is impossible to suppose a greater degree of liberty in living."

By this time there was another war to commemorate, and the Crimea memorial was erected opposite Waterloo Place, cast from cannon captured at Sevastopol. Beside it is a statue of Florence Nightingale with her famous lamp, the only woman among so many male heroes. In due course this al-fresco pantheon would include Scott of the Antarctic, sculpted by his wife Kate, John Franklin of the North West Passage, and that most clubbable of monarchs, Edward VII. A bird's eye view of the square from the top of Benjamin Dean Wyatt's Grand Old Duke of York column is not, however, possible as an internal staircase to its viewing platform has long since closed.

When the United Service Club was taken over by the Institute of Directors in 1972, it was on the understanding that the interior would not be altered. In the Athenaeum, too, though frequently redecorated, little has changed. The chair is preserved in which Charles Dickens sat, conjuring stories about the state of impoverished Londoners, and the club is remembered by literary historians as the place where Dickens and Anthony Trollope made up after a long-standing feud.

Membership is still limited to the select, and these have included more than fifty Nobel Prize winners. Margaret Thatcher remains the only prime minister not to have been invited to join: the men-only rule was not abandoned by the Athenaeum until 2002. Yet the DJ Jimmy Savile was let in, proposed by the late Cardinal Basil Hume. If the serial sex offender had been blackballed, then the Cardinal, who was Archbishop of Westminster at the time, might have been obliged to step down, and that would have caused a real scandal.

LORD'S HALLOWED GROUND

Every sport has its hallowed ground, a place to go to chant anthems, sing praises and issue curses. For London's football clubs, it is their long-standing home grounds. Wembley Stadium, in whatever shape or form, has been sacred since the 1920s; Twickenham Stadium, second in size only to Wembley, is for those whose religion is rugby; tennis fans congregate at Wimbledon; and when it comes to cricket, the name not to take in vain is Lord's.

Thomas Lord opened his first cricket ground with the establishment of the **Marylebone Cricket Club** in 1787, and it moved to its present site on the northwest side of Regent's Park in 1814. The MCC set down the rules of cricket, and laid down the first rules of lawn tennis, too.

The £500-a-year membership has always been something to boast about, not least by sporting the brash red-and-gold ('egg and bacon') striped blazer and tie. Non-playing prospective members must be eighteen years old before they can apply, and there is currently a twenty-three-year waiting list, so it is not surprising that the average age of the 20,000 members is sixty-seven. It was only in 1999 that women were allowed into the club, which is still ninety percent male.

Steeped in tradition, Lord's hosts not only Test matches and county matches for Middlesex, its home ground, but also games that confirm an English elite. The annual Gentlemen versus Players match had its day in 1962, but the Oxford and Cambridge match is still played every year, as is the game between Eton and Harrow, a school team that in 1805, the year of Trafalgar, included Lord Byron. He scored seven runs in the first innings, two in the second, using a runner on account of his club foot, and took one wicket. The Harrow team lost by an innings and two runs.

Though the ground is hallowed, it is not ideal. It has the smallest of England's Test cricket pitches; it slopes from north to south, dropping 6ft 8in (2m), and until resurfaced in the early 21st century the outfield could become waterlogged. The pitch is oriented north-east to south-west and there are twenty-one, 22-yard batting strips that take their turn through the season that lasts from April to September and involves about eighty games. For the rest of the year the ground lies fallow. Nothing happens. The MCC fields its own teams, and the complex includes a Nursery Ground and squash courts. There is also a museum, library and shop, which are open year-round.

The **Pavilion** at Lord's is as renowned as the grounds. It was built in 1890 by the theatre architect Thomas Verity, creator of the sumptuous Criterion restaurant in Piccadilly. It has a suitable Edwardian gaiety about it, the warm terracotta offset by fancy white cast-iron railings and elegant, if uncomfortable, slatted benches. Its principal feature is the Long

Room, where members can watch the game, and anybody can book the room for a wedding or enjoy Sunday tea accompanied by a string quartet.

The walls of this elegant function room are lined with paintings of matches and players. Among them is Thomas Lord, the Yorkshire-born professional cricketer and vintner, whose wine shop stood at the entrance to his first cricket ground. Players' dressing rooms are on the floor above, and they must pass through the Long Room to reach the pitch, using a central door. It means that they will get the close-up approval, or otherwise, of members. It is traditional to give a batsman a polite round of applause at the end of his innings, but when Ian Botham returned to the Long Room after his second duck against Australia in 1981, backs were turned, murmurs were growled and heads hid in newspapers to show their displeasure.

An emblem of the club is the wind vane figure of Father Time, dressed as an umpire, removing bails from stumps at the end of play. It was a gift from Herbert Baker, architect of the original **Grandstand** on the north side of the pitch, replaced in 1998 with a building by Nicholas Grimshaw. Baker had worked around the Commonwealth, in Delhi with Lutyens, in South Africa, Kenya and Australia, and he designed South Africa House in Trafalgar Square.

The south side is where visitors might glimpse Mick Jagger in a private box owned by the late American-born philanthopist Sir John Paul Getty. The oil millionaire was a neighbour of Jagger in Chelsea and one day, the story goes, he dropped round to find out what all the excited noise was: it was Jagger and friends watching cricket on television. Getty, who took out British citizenship in 1997, became hooked and built an idyllic cricket ground in his country estate at Wormsley in Buckinghamshire, became president of Surrey Cricket Club and bought *Wisden*, the cricketers' annual Bible. He also paid for the **Mound Stand** at Lord's, designed by Michael Hopkins with a tented canopy and seventy-two hospitality boxes that can be rented for £200,000 a year. Getty died in 2003, and his box has remained in the family's hands.

Dominating the pitch is the Media Centre, the giant silver pod opposite the Pavilion at the Nursery end, completed in 1999. This two-storey ship-shaped aluminium structure was the inspiration of the Czech architect Jan Kaplicky, who over the years had worked with Denys Lasdun, Renzo Piano, Richard Rogers and Norman Foster before starting his own practice, Future Systems. No traditional builder could be found for the monocoque construction, which eventually relied on the skills of boat yards in Cornwall and Holland.

W.G. Grace, the hero of Lord's, and of English cricket, is remembered in the name of the main gate, next to the **Lord's Tavern**, and in a statue behind the Pavilion in a green space enjoyed by picnicking visitors. Other batting and bowling heroes of Test matches played at the grounds are commemorated in Honour Boards in the players' dressing rooms in the Pavilion. Batsmen who have knocked up centuries and bowlers who have taken five or more wickets in a single match contain some unfamiliar names, while some familiar names are absent. Sachin Tendulkar, for instance, recognised as India's greatest batsman, never made a century at Lord's and has to be content with a temple in India, which film star Manoj Tiwari began building for him after his retirement in 2013, declaring the cricketer to be "an incarnation of God in the world of cricket".

Other heroes are remembered in the **MCC Museum**, said to be the largest sporting museum in the world. This is where the ashes are kept. The symbolic shrine is barely three inches tall, a terracotta perfume jar in the shape of a Greek urn containing the remains of bails burned on an irrelevant pitch in Melbourne

Their story is convoluted. When England first lost to Australia in 1882, the match was not at Lord's but at the Oval. The following day the *Sporting Times* contained an unsigned announcement:

"In Affectionate Remembrance of English Cricket, which died at the Oval on 29th August, 1882, Deeply lamented by a large circle of sorrowing friends and acquaintances. RIP. N.B, – The body will be cremated and the ashes taken to Australia."

There was no cremation and no ashes but the idea caught the imagination of the public who followed the English team as they shortly afterwards set off for Australia. During their successful tour, their captain, the Honourable Ivo Bligh, the future 8th Earl of Darnley, was a dinner guest of Sir William Clarke, president of another MCC, the Melbourne Cricket Club. On her own initiative, it seems, Lady Jane Clarke had a pair of bails burned and the ashes placed in an urn-shaped perfume bottle which she presented to Bligh as a playful souvenir. Her co-conspirator was Florence Morphy, whom Bligh later married, and the couple kept the urn until Bligh died in 1927, when it was presented to the MCC, where for some years it was displayed in the Long Room.

The urn has remained at Lord's ever since. However, in 1997, following five successive 'Ashes' wins by the Australians, there was a call for them to be returned to Australia. Claiming the relic was too fragile to travel, the MCC agreed to create an actual trophy, modelled on the original. Made from crystal glass, and donated by Waterford, it is etched with a copy of the verse that Lady Clarke pasted on the urn before it left for England. Titled *Ashes*, it had appeared in *Melbourne Punch* and it included the names of England's finest. It can still be seen stuck onto the original.

When Ivo goes back with the urn, the urn;
Studds, Steel, Read and Tylecote return, return;
The welkin will ring loud,
The great crowd will feel proud,
Seeing Barlow and Bates with the urn, the urn;
And the rest coming home with the urn.

In the meantime, whatever the outcome of the Ashes, the urn remains on view in the Museum, the most sacred object on this hallowed ground.

PATRON SAINTS
OF THE ARTS

The fastest selling tickets to any show at the **Victoria and Albert Museum** were for the David Bowie exhibition in 2013. The world's largest museum of decorative arts and design is such a fusty looking old building that it seems an unlikely place to exhibit the heights of celebrity style. But the museum is never out of fashion, and on Late Night Fridays, the last in each month, some of London's best-dressed students come out to play in the spacious galleries of South Kensington's grandest building.

This storehouse of costumes and textiles is also a vast treasure trove for which the word 'eclectic' seems too inadequate a description. The three million or so items in its collections range from the monumental sculptures of the Cast Courts to tiny Egyptian perfume jars from 1400BC, and in a partnership with the Royal Institute of British Architects it has imported the library from RIBA's 1930s headquarters in Portland Place and opened a permanent gallery of architecture.

In trying to strike a balance between oak-panelled authority and street fun, the museum often attracts complaints. Are Kylie Minogue's hot pants really worth exhibiting? What would Queen Victoria and her consort, Prince Albert, have thought?

The celebrities and heroes of Victoria's day can be seen on the Cromwell Road façade of the main, 1909 building. A vast stone imperial crown with Ionic pillars tops this later part of the museum, which was designed by Aston Webb, who was responsible for giving Buckingham Palace and the Mall their present look. Beside the first-floor windows here and around the corner in Exhibition Road, thirty-six male British artistic figures stand on plinths like so many saints on the west front of a cathedral: six architects, ten painters, six sculptors and ten craftsmen.

London's medieval guilds often enrolled their patron saints from the church with which they were connected, while some saints are associated with trades. In 2012, for example, the recently founded Worshipful Company of Constructors adopted St Thomas, patron saint of architects and builders. The only saint among the V&A's devotional ensemble is St Dunstan, builder of monasteries, Archbishop of Canterbury and blacksmith, who, legend tells, tweaked the devil's nose with red-hot tongs. He was also a jeweller, and is patron saint of silversmiths and goldsmiths, which explains why all hallmarks are dated each year from May 19, because that is his saint's day.

Several other figures on the Aston Webb building are not instantly recognisable. The painters are familiar, and so is William Morris, the leading figure of the Arts & Crafts movement and inspiration for the architects who founded the Art Workers' Guild. But craftsmen such as the 13th-century sculptor William Torell and the master ironmonger Roger Payne need Googling. Sir Christopher Wren has a place, but no plinth was kept for Captain Francis Fowke and his successor Major-General Henry Young Darracott Scott of the Royal Engineers, the original architects of the South Kensington museums.

There is, however, a memorial to Henry Cole, the man who realised Prince Albert's mission to educate the people of Britain through the institutions of 'Albertopolis'. A mosaic portrait by his niece, Florence Cole, among the high Victorian tiles of the Ceramic Staircase shows the far-sighted gaze and distinctive white chin beard of this tireless organiser. Cole was a full-time civil servant, part-time industrial designer and leading figure in the Royal Society of Arts where he encountered Prince Albert whom he helped mount the **Great Exhibition** of 1851.

Hyde Park's gigantic showcase trumpeting art and manufacturing had many imitators, and was such a success that it not only paid for Albertopolis, but it is still handing out funds today. Land was bought from Kensington Gardens to Cromwell Road in Brompton, renamed South Kensington to give it cachet. Joseph Paxton's Crystal Palace that housed the exhibition was moved to Sydenham under Fowke's supervision, and on the east side of Exhibition Road the South Kensington Museum was established in new iron galleries that housed exhibits left over from 1851, swelled by further donations. Designed by Prince Albert and clad in corrugated iron, the three galleries nicknamed the 'Brompton Boilers' would eventually be removed by Henry Scott to Bethnal Green to become the V&A in East London, now the **Museum of Childhood**.

A follow-up exhibition, ten years after the first, was planned on the west side of Exhibition Road, where the **Natural History Museum** now stands. Fowke, as chief architect, had a great deal of work to do. A ramrod-backed officer with lashings of moustaches, he came from an Irish military family. At the time he was taken on by Cole, over whom he towered, he had just completed the interior of the National Gallery in Dublin and would go on to build the National Museum of Scotland in Edinburgh. He invented a bellows camera, inflatable pontoons and a novel umbrella. Henry Cole's bright ideas included the first Christmas cards and the first children's illustrated book publishing house. It was a meeting of constantly curious minds. The son of an army officer, Cole was largely self-taught. He favoured engineers over architects, whom he thought were too stuck in the past. Engineers had, after all, helped to build an empire, with bridges, barracks and fortifications that often needed a great deal of ingenuity. They were good at forward planning and could complete projects on time and on, if not under, budget. Often in the saddle, they were distinguished by their spurs, which still add a dash to their dress uniforms.

Following the acquisition of land, the west side of Exhibition Road was largely given over to the **Royal Horticultural Society Gardens**, and one of Fowke's first buildings was a Crystal-Palace style conservatory on the north side. This would provide the original entrance lobby for the **Royal Albert Hall**. When South Kensington Underground station was built, the tunnel that now serves the V&A and Science Museum led to a colonnade in the gardens and to the conservatory, so visitors could reach the Hall on rainy days without getting wet. An idea of these engineers' ambitions can be gleaned from the

Royal Albert Hall's unprecedented dome. The elliptical iron frame was constructed in Manchester, dismantled and transported south where it was placed on blocks on scaffolding erected around the Hall's roof. Nobody knew what would happen when the blocks were removed, so the building was evacuated as Henry Scott and a colleague knocked out the wedges. The 400-ton iron structure settled into place just half an inch off target.

Fowke's design for the Royal Albert Hall, an unprecedented indoor arena based on the Roman amphitheatre in Nîmes, which he had visited with Cole, had beaten off all competitors, including Sir George Gilbert Scott. But when Prince Albert died in 1861, blamed in part by his grieving widow on the amount of time he had spent in the RHS gardens, the architect of the St Pancras Midland Grand Hotel had the consolation of a commission to build the **Albert Memorial** in Kensington Gardens opposite. Albert might not have approved of this extraordinary gilded shrine, because it took funds away from his pet projects, and it wasn't until 1865 that the Queen approved Fowke's plans for the Hall. That December, however, Fowkes died from a ruptured blood vessel, at the same age as Prince Albert, just forty-two.

Cole missed the resourceful and inventive architect. "England has lost a man who felt the spirit of his age," he said, "and was daring enough to venture beyond the beaten path of conventionalism."

Fowke had put a stamp firmly on the South Kensington museums. He had designed all the galleries around the central quadrangle based on a northern Italian Renaissance style, with distinctive façades of brick and terracotta. On the north side of the square double bronze doors by James Gamble were intended as the museum's main entrance, leading to the wonderfully decorated Refreshment Rooms, highlights of the Arts and Crafts movement, still in use today.

Incorporated into the complex was the South Kensington Museum Schools, now the **Henry Cole Wing**. This magnificent Renaissance building with an attic loggia and corner pavilions, stands out among the mix of buildings in Exhibition Road. Henry Scott, who had been on the committee carrying out Fowke's designs, completed the work, adding his own interpretations and building the Royal Albert Hall to which he added an 800ft (245m) terraccotta frieze made by students at the South Kensington Museum.

At the time of his death, Fowke was "appreciating the spirit of both Gothic and Renaissance, and was on the threshold of introducing a novel style of architecture", according to Cole. How that novel style might have evolved had Fowke lived another forty-two years will never be known. South Kensington would certainly have looked different. Instead of Aston Webb's cool and imperious building there might have been a more original 270ft (82m) frontage on Cromwell Road, complementing Fowke's design for the Natural History Museum, which had already been accepted by the time of his death but was never realised. An aricle *The Builder* lamented its loss:

"Fowke's natural aptitude for the art [of architecture] enabled him to realise this very beautiful design. It was neither Grecian nor Gothic, but thoroughly 19th century, and had he lived... his building would have marked an epoch in the history of architecture in this country."

It was left to Alfred Waterhouse, a prolific architect who had moved his practice to London from Manchester ten years earlier, to make a name for himself with his own distinctive Natural History Museum building.

Neither Fowke nor Scott have their statues on a plinth, and there is no sign in the V&A of monuments to either man, though somewhere among the museum's millions of objects is a gilt-bronze bust of Fowke by Thomas Woolner.

The Royal Engineers have not forgotten "the most brilliant constructive architect the Corp has ever produced", and there is a bust of him in the Royal Engineers Museum in Gillingham, Kent. Every year a Fowke medal is struck in bronze for the most promising student on the Royal School of Military Engineering's Clerk of Works course, the foundation of all building projects.

ACADEMIC HEIGHTS

The **National Gallery**, that Classical temple to European art that overlooks Trafalgar Square, has a twin just over a mile away in the Wilkins Building of **University College London**. Students flock like starlings to sit and chat on the broad steps that rise to a familiar portico with ten Corinthian columns and a main hall topped by a dome. The architect of both buildings was William Wilkins, the son of a Norwich builder and theatre manager, whose architectural career began at Cambridge where he had studied mathematics.

At the age of twenty-three Wilkins was awarded a scholarship that took him to the Ancient Greek colonies in Italy and Sicily, which led to the publication of *The Antiquities of Magna Graecia* and a life-long attachment to Greek Revival. He completed the University College building in 1828, four years before starting on the National Gallery. University College is London's oldest university. Described by the educator and Rugby School headmaster Thomas

Arnold as "that godless institution of Gower Street", it was founded to counter the elitism of Oxford and Cambridge where the prerequisites of wealth, male gender and a Protestant religion excluded the bulk of the population. The founders' inclusive ideology had a hero and champion in the reformer Jeremy Bentham whose shrine remains one of London's great curiosities. His skeleton, wrapped in hay to fill his clothes, sits alarmingly upright, fully dressed in distinctive waistcoat and broad-brimmed hat, in a booth in the South Cloister of the Wilkins Building. The original preserved head, frequently carted off by prankster students, is now kept elsewhere and has been replaced by a waxwork, from which some of of Bentham's real hair sprouts. A startling figure to encounter, he still has a role to play at the University: on special occasions the 'auto-icon' is called upon to attend meetings at which he is minuted as being present but not voting.

The other pioneering London university was **King's College** in the Strand, and in 1836 the two came together under the umbrella of the University of London. Much as Oxford and Cambridge universities are each made up of a number of colleges, the University of London acts as administrative centre and clearing house for the city's otherwise self-governing colleges. There are eighteen of them, plus ten smaller institutions, and they are attended by around 170,000 students. Another 50,000 students are signed up to its international programme.

The University of London's home is Bloomsbury where it owns 180 buildings and four squares. Here its great temple, the heart of London learning, is **Senate House**. There is a North American look to this Art Deco skyscraper, rising sheer behind an open courtyard, a mammoth, geometrical cliff-face seen from Tottenham Court Road. For twenty years it was the tallest secular building in the city, and it would not look out of place in Chicago or New York. This has nothing to do with the fact that the Rockefeller Foundation provided money to build it, nor that the word 'senate' is often associated with the US government, and more to do with the fact that its architect had spent a year in America on a RIBA scholarship.

In fact the building could not be more British. *Keep Calm and Carry On,* a phrase that epitomises the country's spirit, was coined here during the Second World War when it was commandeered by the Ministry of Information to manage propaganda. Half London's non-combatant cultural figures came through its doors: Lord Clark was making films, Dylan Thomas was writing them, John Betjeman encountered, in the catering department, Joan Hunter Dunn (*Miss J. Hunter Dunn, Miss J. Hunter Dunn,/Furnish'd and burnish'd by Aldershot sun/What strenuous singles we played after tea/We in the tournament – you against me!*). The building also inspired George Orwell's Ministry of Truth in *Nineteen Eighty-Four.* The tedious meetings that he attended, he said, were "the worst thing in the world", though his Room 101 was actually based on a ministry building at 55 Portland Place.

When war broke out, Senate House had only been open for a couple of years. The site was chosen after the University of London had been wandering the city for almost a century, from Somerset House to South Kensington via Burlington Gardens. The Lancastrian architect Charles Holden, a tee-totalling Quaker, was selected from a short list of four over a black-tie dinner at the Athenaeum, a far cry from his roots as the son of a bankrupt Bolton draper. Apart from the experience of his American sojourn, his pared down, Modernist style had been developed when he worked with Lutyens in the War Graves Commission. By the time of his appointment, he was best known for working with London Transport's Frank Pick, and his credentials included some elegant Underground stations. Most spectacularly, he had designed London's first skyscraper, another Art Deco blockbuster, at **55 Broadway**, London Transport's Headquarter above St James's Park tube station. Until Senate House was completed half a dozen years later, this was the tallest building in London. In 2015 it will go the way of the PLA Building and many other national treasures: London Underground staff will slink off to some uninspiring box and the building will then be turned into luxury apartments.

Senate House, on the other hand, seems destined for a long life. Sited across eight acres immediately behind London's great temple to culture, the **British Museum**, it had to make its mark. In fact, the 219ft- (67m)-tall building is scaled down from Holden's original designs, and there were insufficient funds for the sculptures by Eric Gill, Jacob Epstein and Henry Moore that he would have liked to have seen adorn the building, as they had done at 55 Broadway.

William Beveridge, the forward-looking Vice-Chancellor, is credited with much of the inspiration behind the building, which he saw as *"something that could not have been built by any earlier generation than this… an academic island in swirling tides of traffic, a world of learning in a world of affairs"*. But it is the Principal of the University who is often better remembered today, when it is gleefully pointed out to freshers that his ghost still haunts the building. Sir Edwin Deller was killed when a workman's barrow fell on him while he was showing visitors around the rising tower. He had taken them in the lift up to the first floor, then descended again, but a workman did not realise that the lift had departed, and he pushed his barrow into the empty shaft at the bottom of which stood the party. None escaped injury and Deller died four days later. The son of a Devon carpenter, he had a law degree from King's College and had been made an Honorary Bencher of the Inner Temple. His funeral was held in the Templar church, and a death notice in the *Times* contained a verse that imagined Senate House as his memorial:

> *I find him in the wonder of his Tower,*
> *That monstrous, beautiful and bloody Tower,*
> *His wordless monument, which seems to say,*
> *"For this he worked and planned and gave*
> *his life,*
> *Then took his wages – Death – and went*
> *his way."*

The building was constructed of Portland stone without the help of a steel frame, as Holden wanted it to last five hundred years. Among its innovations were electric central heating, a discreet system that heats wall panels, and early use of fluorescent lights. Holden was an Arts and Crafts devotee, and he paid close attention to the details of the interior. The buffed and polished travertine marble reflects the ample quantities of daylight, which bounces off brass fittings and gold leaf, and it is as crisp and sharp today as it must have been when it opened for business on the centenary of London University's founding, in 1936. The interior halls and rooms are generously proportioned, particularly the main Crush Hall on the first and second floors, which is used for ceremonies. Other rooms and halls are available for hire.

Senate House Library is concerned with the arts, humanities and social sciences, and occupies the top fifteen floors. The London Building Act of 1894 forbade skyscrapers this tall as they would be out of reach of firemen's ladders, but the act was circumvented as these floors were designated for uses as archives. More than 3 million books are kept here, plus 13,000 political pamphlets and posters, some by former students.

South Block Café, with a door opposite the back entrance of the British Museum in Montague Street, is open from 8.30 in the morning until 6pm, but closed at weekends. It is a low-key alternative to the high-volume café in the museum's rotunda, and an ideal place for a quiet moment with a book.

TEMPLES OF CULTURE

The two great arts centres in London, the **Barbican** and **South Bank**, were both built in the second half of the 20th century and they have many things in common, not least an astonishing amount of opprobrium heaped upon them over the years. But they have many fans and many differences, too.

The **Barbican Arts Centre** is Europe's largest multi-arts venue. It lies by a lake at the heart of the City's 35-acre Barbican development that took nearly thirty years to plan and build. It went through many changes of ideas, starting in the period of Modernism and ending with Post-Modernism, and among fancies that it entertained was the use of Temple Bar from Fleet Street as a grand entrance and the re-siting of the Coal Exchange's highly decorated interior, which was being dismantled in Thames Street.

Central to the architects' thinking was the expectation that people coming to the arts centre would arrive by car. This may well have been true just after the war. For example, John James Joass's Art Deco **Lex Garage** in Brewer Street, Soho, now a listed building, had been designed to serve West End theatre audiences and it had a canteen where chauffeurs could spin out the evening, as well as two ladies' changing rooms.

By the time the Barbican Arts Centre was completed in 1982, however, many people had given up their cars, not to mention their chauffeurs, and instead of arriving at what was supposed to be the main entrance in a subterranean drop-off point, they struggled to read the signs that would guide them from Barbican and Moorgate stations. This brought them through the bleak Highwalks to the Lakeside entrance at the back of the building by the long, shallow waters above the tunnel of the Metropolitan Line.

The Highwalks were essential to the Barbican development, which involved more than 2,000 flats in three towers and many blocks. The area had been devastated in the war, and the local population had dwindled to little more than a thousand. Peter Chamberlin, Geoffrey Powell and Christof Bon, who had been responsible for the colourful **Golden Lane Estate** on the north side of the Barbican, were appointed by the City as principal architects. They had been teachers at Kingston Polytechnic and they came together for what was to become a lifetime's work.

The flats, with between one and five bedrooms, included penthouses and even a row of mews-type houses. They were designed purely for rental at a relatively inexpensive rate to attract a residential population back to the City, and although privately owned, they were included in Margaret Thatcher's 'right to buy' scheme when many of the tenants made a killing.

This area was always known as the Barbican, taking its name from the Roman fortress that stood on this northwest corner of their city of Londinium.

The development gave it a newly embattled air, with arrow slits for windows in its heavy walls, squat towers and crenellations. Such fortifications make it look inwards, turning its back on the rest of the City, though the idea had been that the raised Highwalks would continue into the surrounding streets to elevate and integrate a large part of central London, leaving traffic to pass beneath. But this never happened here nor anywhere else around the world where the experiment was attempted.

Included in the Barbican site is the **Museum of London**, the **City of London School for Girls** – the boys' equivalent was moved to a new site by the Thames – and the **Guildhall School of Music and Drama**. The London Symphony Orchestra is the resident band.

The Stalls Foyer entrance to the Arts Centre in the motorists' tunnel leading off Silk Street is not much used by audiences now. In early 2006 a street-level entrance opened in Silk Street beside the tunnel. At the same time the focal point of the interior, the great well from which all its facilities were accessed, was bridged with a new floor that allowed visitors to walk directly across the building from the new Silk Street Foyer to the Lakeside Foyer. But signage remains hopeless, and the Centre is a challenge to navigate. It is not immediately clear, for example, how to reach the excellent Barbican Library, bounteous in books about music and London, which is visible in the main foyer. The secret is to head for the stairs near the Lakeside Foyer where the activities of each floor is listed.

Deep in the bowels of the theatre at Level −2 is a cinema and The Pit, the theatre originally occupied by the Royal Shakespeare Company and so far beneath the ground, and so well protected, that it could be used as a nuclear bunker. In the opposite direction, the flytower above the main theatre has been softened with foliage and surrounded by a glass Conservatory with walkways, an aviary and terrapins. This seemingly secret hideaway is open to the public on Sunday afternoons.

Two of the Centre's cinemas are now in Beech Street, moved there from the residential area behind the sculpture garden that occupies the roof of the main concert hall, as they disturbed the neighbours. The Curve is an art gallery wrapped around the main concert hall, inside an outer wall installed by Ove Arup to make sure the whole thing didn't collapse.

Ove Arup was a key figure in London's Modernist buildings. Born in Newcastle to Norwegian and Danish parents and educated in Denmark, he was a master of structural engineering who specialised in concrete, designing the Mulberry caissons used for the D-Day landing in Normandy, and Sydney Opera House. He worked with the Russian emigré Berthold Lubetkin and was equally influential in the city's 20th-century architecture.

Concrete is the main building material of the Barbican, its rough concrete aggregate flecked with black chips of Welsh granite. Everything was created on site, and some of the pillars were made to look more natural by roughing them up with jack-hammers and pneumatic drills, an almost medieval way of working that produced its own particular geology. Never in need of cleaning, the fabric has not discoloured, and by and large the whole place has weathered well, benefitting from the City of London's commitment to proper upkeep. The whole development is now Grade II listed, which means none of the residents can paint their doors or windows a different colour or install double glazing.

Brutalism was introduced on the South Bank when the **Queen Elizabeth Hall**, **Purcell Room** and **Hayward Gallery** were built between 1967 and 1968 under Hubert Bennett, head of the London County Council's architect's department. The word is derived from the French *béton brut*, meaning 'raw concrete', and it is used to describe the way in which the pattern of the timbers imprinted by the shuttering of the cement remains untouched as a natural surface. Concrete aggregate panels, echoing the Barbican, were also used in these buildings, which were the last elements of the South Bank Centre that had begun with the **Royal Festival Hall**. This was the centrepiece of the 1951 **Festival of Britain**, designed under the London County Council's chief architect, Leslie Martin, who was in his thirties. All of the architects, artists and designers employed for the Festival under Hugh Casson had to be under the age of forty-five. One of the RFH's associate architects was Peter Moro from Heidelberg, who was mainly responsible for the hall's interior design. In 1936 at the age of twenty-five, he had fled Germany penniless and found work in London with Berthold Lubetkin. At the outbreak of war, he had been interned as an enemy alien on the Isle of Wight. He would go on to design the Nottingham Playhouse and the Theatre Royal in Plymouth.

Post-war London had no surviving large concert hall, and the RFH was built to replace Queen's Hall in Langham Place, opposite the BBC's Broadcasting House, which had been bombed to bits on the same violent night in May 1941 when the Great Synagogue was destroyed and the Temple of Mithras revealed. It was in the Queen's Hall that the Henry Wood Promenade concerts had begun, but after the war they chose to resume the Proms in Kensington's Royal Albert Hall where they would become the world's largest classical music series.

Like the Barbican, the South Bank Centre had difficulty in working out where its main entrance should be. It had been planned for the north side, in Belvedere Road, where the Canteen restaurant is now situated. Instead, it went for the Highwalk option with an approach through the Shell Centre from Waterloo Station, and the main entrance on the riverside terrace. In 1999 the Highwalk was dismantled and its Thames-side profile was enhanced with a new entrance among a parade of restaurants.

The South Bank Centre continues to come up with innovative ideas to keep everyone entertained, including a rooftop garden and vegetable plots above the Queen Elizabeth Hall, and the **Room for London** by David Kohn Architects and artist Fiona Banner, that could be hired for the night with what must be one of the best views in London. There are also summer sandy beaches and fountains, Christmas fairs and a skateboard park championed by Mayor Johnson. On any evening of the week there might be small groups of actors or dancers rehearsing, drawing lessons or knitting clubs gathered in the public spaces. The Sunday afternoon free concerts in the Clore Ballroom are popular, and the vocal glass lift in which a chorus rises with each floor is a typical delight.

The Festival of Britain had dropped like a great cultural boulder on the South Bank, sending out ripples that affected the whole promenade from Westminster to London Bridge. Though the South

Bank Centre claims to be the largest single-run arts centre in the world, most Londoners regard the South Bank as more than this one complex. On the west side is the **London Eye**. On the east side are the **British Film Institute**, the **National Theatre**, the galleries of Coin Street and the **Oxo Tower**, **Tate Modern**, **Shakespeare's Globe** and the **Sam Wanamaker Playhouse**. This feast of culture in less than a mile makes the South Bank London's most popular outdoor space.

The National Theatre has perhaps been the most controversial block, derided, not surprisingly, by Prince Charles as looking like a nuclear power station. For others it is a sublime work of Modernism with a succession of clean lines, the horizontal terraces and vertical flytowers making bold geometric shapes. Brutalism is at its best in the interior, where spotlights on pillars and stairways clearly reveal the knots and grain of the timber in which the concrete was cast. It provides drama rather than comfort. Its architect, Denys Lasdun, was a Londoner, the son of a builder and a pianist. He says that the Olivier, largest of the National's three auditoria, was inspired by the Greek theatre at Epidaurus.

"Concrete is very intractable," Lasdun told the National's director, Peter Hall, during its construction in the 1970s. "But it can be a beautiful material if it is used in the way its own nature intends it to be used. It is a sort of sculpture that you can only do with reinforced concrete, but you need to work to a certain scale. It is not a cosy little material."

Both the Barbican and the South Bank have been bold experiments that have endured. But they have also left seeds of disquiet, a restlessness, and plans seem always to be afoot to resolve perceived issues, while endeavouring to keep the performance spaces up to scratch on a world stage.

Any proposed developments face an uphill struggle. In 1994 Richard Rogers' idea for a Crystal Palace, a glass enclosure enveloping much of the South Bank, was one of ten short-listed but unfulfilled plans. In 2010 Haworth Tompkins' scheme for a £70million revamp of the National Theatre were attacked by members of Lasdun's original team, and in 2014 a Festival Wing extension was turned down by Mayor Johnson in a populace move, as it would involve the skate park moving 100 yards west. Everyone, it seems, has a strong idea about what could and should be done with these much appreciated public spaces.

It is, however, difficult to find detractors from Joanna Lumley's bright idea, realised by Thomas Heartherwick, for a pedestrian **Garden Bridge** connecting the temples of culture on the South Bank with the Knights Templars' Temple opposite.

THE BUDDHIST TEMPLE

It is hard to imagine the saffron-robed monks of the **Wat Buddhapadipa** in Wimbledon setting out on their morning alms round, their sandals scrunching on front drives in the expectation of a little sustenance for the day. In these streets of millionaires' mansions doors are firmly shut, fences are high and the traffic is so negligible that learner drivers are brought here for instruction. Such a hushed atmosphere is ideal for meditation.

The Council of Thai Buddhist Monks of the United Kingdom of Great Britain and Northern Ireland, practitioners of Theravada Buddhism to which 95 percent of the Thai population adheres, has its headquarters in one such mansion. Unlike its neighbours', the gates here are always open.

This is the main building of the *wat,* or monastery complex, the home of an abbot and half a dozen monks. The yellow brick, double-fronted building was featured in *Ideal Home* in 1931 five years after it was completed and outwardly it seems little changed. With four acres of gardens, it was called Barrogill then, named after Britain's northernmost castle, to which Queen Elizabeth the Queen Mother retreated on becoming a widow, changing its name to the Castle of Mey. A royal connection remains, except that now the monarch is the King of Thailand, patron of the *wat*, which started life in Richmond in 1965 and moved here in 1976 when a typical Thai temple, an *ubosot,* was constructed in the grounds. Set among contrasting dark cedars and guarded by fanciful lions, it is a twinkling jewel box dripping in red and gold, with glass chips that play with the passing light. This perfect Thai temple is the only one of its kind in Europe. Used for prayers and ceremonal occasions, the white-walled T-shaped building has four gable roofs topped with *chofahs,* golden finials flying skywards representing mythical birds.

The main space is the Shrine Room where a highly decorated altar centres on three images of Buddha and his disciples. Behind the main golden Buddha is one in black bronze, a gift from the king, brought here from the original Richmond temple, while a small gold Buddha was donated by Queen Elizabeth II, who had been given it on an earlier trip to Bangkok.

But it is the murals of the Life of Buddha that really catch the eye. Surreal and somewhat cartoonish, the twenty-eight scenes painted between 1984 and 1992 cover the walls with myriad traditional and contemporary figures. Among images of the sleeping Buddha are a space rocket, Superman and Ninja Turtles, and in the crowded scenes are such recognisable faces as David Hockney, Vincent van Gogh, Margaret Thatcher and the King of Thailand himself. The project was carried out by more than two dozen artists, all recent graduates, led by Chalermchai Kositpipat and Panya Vijinthanasarn, who had just completed a degree course at London's

Slade School of Fine Arts. For their labours they were paid nothing but their keep.

The murals have upset traditionalists, but King Bhumibol Adulyadej, also known as King Rama IX, who came to the throne in 1947 and is the world's longest-reigning monarch, loved them. He is something of a dab hand at art himself, not to say a jazz trumpeter and Elvis fan, and he has said that the murals represent the art of his reign.

The *ubosot* is open at weekends, and there is a basement room for meditation classes. Otherwise visitors are free to wander round the grounds where contemplative paths, signposted with sayings of the Buddha, open onto a grove for communal meditation. Even the carp in the lake seem to be meditating, though they are energised with oxygen through a contraption designed by the king himself and installed in 2012.

Wat Buddhapadipa (The Light of Buddhism Monastery) is ten minutes' walk from both Wimbledon Common and the **All-England Lawn Tennis Club**. During the hectic Wimbledon fortnight it can be a place for escape. Serbia's Novak Djokovic, the 2011 men's champion, usually stays in a house nearby, and he has spoken of his visits to the temple.

"I can't talk much about it," he said. "But I can just say that it is a very calm and very beautiful environment where I like to spend time."

LONDON CENTRAL MOSQUE

Londoners had never seen a burqa on their streets until the 1970s. They arrived with Arab money that gushed from the oil crisis brought about when OPEC, the Organisation for the Petroleum Exporting Countries, responded to the Arab-Israeli war by imposing an oil embargo, which pushed up the price of their most valuable raw material. Every taxi driver in town knew how many dollars would buy a barrel on any given day. Sheikhs hired whole floors in Park Lane hotels, their black-robed women created a sales boom in Oxford Street, and mansions in Kensington were snapped up. There was investment and philanthropy, too, both in their own countries and abroad, and architects found new patrons. In London, King Fahd of Saudi Arabia and Zayed bin Sultan Al Nahyan, emir of Abu Dhabi and first president of the United Arab Emirates, used some of their millions to fund the **London Central Mosque** in Regent's Park.

The two-and-a-half-acre site already belonged to the Islamic community. The **Islamic Cultural Centre** had been opened by George VI in 1944 on land donated by the wartime government of Winston

Churchill in recognition of the thousands of Muslims serving with the British forces. More Muslims than Christians lived in the Empire then, many of them among the 2,500,000 who had joined the Indian Army, the largest volunteer force in history that included recruits from what is now Bangladesh and Pakistan. But it wasn't until this generous funding arrived some thirty years later that a fitting mosque could be built.

Sir Frederick Gibberd, the architect chosen for the project, had a number of English religious houses in his large portfolio, including a cathedral (Liverpool Metropolitan), Benedictine monastery (Douai Abbey, Berkshire), Baptist Church (Thomas Cooper Memorial Church, Lincoln) and Chapel (St George's at Heathrow, where he had designed the first terminals). Born in Coventry in 1908, he trained in Birmingham and lived for nearly thirty years in Harlow New Town in Essex for which he had been the master planner. A dapper dresser, Gibberd had a bushy moustache and kept his hair at an arty length. Works by John Piper, Henry Moore and Paul Nash no longer hang on the walls of Gibberd House, which is otherwise much as he left it when he died in 1984. The library contains his drawings, including the work on the mosque, and the seven-acre **Gibberd Garden** is open to the public. A clutch of four Greek Coade stone urns and two Portland stone Corinthian columns were salvaged from **Coutts Bank** in the Strand, a Nash building he redeveloped in 1976 with a dramatic glass front and garden atrium.

"I have made a special glade to take them, which I shall plant with cypress trees," he told the local paper when they were erected, not without difficulty, in 1975. "There is a mound of earth in Temple Fields where Harlow had its Roman temple. You could say I have put it up again in my garden."

The challenge posed by the Coutts building had echoes of the one presented by the mosque on which Gibberd was working at around the same time. On the west side of Regent's Park, the new Islamic centre needed to fit in with the buildings that John Nash and Decimus Burton had designed for the Prince Regent, who would become George IV. This Hanoverian monarch had wanted to focus the Classical architecture of the terraces and villas on a palace for himself in the centre of Regent's Park, but financial constraints forced him to make do with Buckingham Palace. Each of Regent's Park's gates is named after one of 'Prinny's' titles, and the cream-coloured Regency buildings look as fresh and fabulous today as they must have done when they had just been completed.

On the west side of the park by Hanover Gate is Hanover Terrace, a temple to aristocratic Regency living. Each of its three Doric porticoes has a pediment and a sculpted tympanum in blue, Wedgwood style, topped with a trio of Muses. Outside, vans of chandelier cleaners can be seen parked in between the latest black Bentley, Maserati and Land Rover. These properties don't often come up for sale but in 2013 one of the pedimented end-of-terrace blocks, with fourteen bedrooms and a garden containing a mews house and a cottage, with two bedrooms in each, was on the market for £34 million.

Nash also planned fifty villas for the park. Only nine of them were built, but in the late 1980s the Crown Estate asked Prince Charles' favourite architect, Quinlan Terry, to build six more. It was a dream commission for Terry, who is so steeped in Classical architecture that he added Doric pillars to No.10 Downing Street when he refurbished it for the prime minister, Margaret Thatcher.

Betweeen these six villas, named Corinthian, Doric, Gothick, Ionic, Tuscan and Veneto, and Hanover Gate there used to be Nash's smallest villa, Albany Cottage. Described on its completion in 1826 as a cottage *ornée*, or possibly a *cottage ornée*, it was later renamed Regent's Lodge, and its last inhabitant was Lady Ribblesdale, the socialite American Ava Lowie Willing, whose first marriage had been to John Jacob Astor who went down on the *Titanic*. Lady Ribblesdale returned to America at the outbreak of war, and the 'cottage' was used as a children's evacuation centre.

It was this property that the government gave to the Muslim community and it functioned as an Islamic Centre with an ever growing congregation until Gibberd came up with a concrete and glass complex to replace it.

Well aware of its position among the surrounding Regency paradigms, and conscious that he was bringing Islamic architecture onto the Western world stage, Gibberd declared: "The shade of Prinny must delight in the prospect of a stately Indo-Saracenic dome floating over a cool white colonnade of Persian pointed arches among the planes of his royal park."

The great copper dome does indeed float over the cool white colonnade, though not quite as brightly as it did at first. Its inspiration is Jerusalem's Dome of the Rock, and beside it a 141ft (43m) minaret, accessed via an internal escalator, stands mute. Prayers are said five times a day, synchronised with the clock at Greenwich Observatory. Beneath the dome, words from the Qu'ran are written around its perimeter above the large, bare square hall, lit by a chandelier. Women are confined to a balcony, and there are separate ablution areas. On Fridays one of the five incumbent *imams* gives a sermon at the golden *mihrab*, and speakers are invited from all over the world.

This is a mainstream, Arab-speaking Sunni mosque, with nearly thirty countries represented on its board of trustees. Shi'as and adherents of other Muslim sects also attend, and its congregation remains the most mixed of all London's mosques. Up to 4,500 can expand to 6,000 or more during holy festivals when they spill into the main courtyard. As an educational centre, it has exhibition rooms in the basement with displays that require closer reading than some of the pupils from London schools, brought in groups, might care to give. The first room explains the importance of Allah and the Prophet Mohammad, the second the achievements of Islam in science and the place of women. The Qu'ran is an immutable text and all *imams* have to learn it by heart, though there are tales of children younger than ten who have mastered it. The language of the Qu'ran is Arabic, and the Islamic Cultural Centre runs language courses alongside study classes. It is also an advice centre, particularly on marital matters, and there is a room for weddings and ceremonies.

Many other mosques and Islamic prayer houses have been built in London since the Regent's Park mosque was completed, some of them much larger. The biggest, the East London Mosque in Whitechapel, dating from 1982 and built on a Second World War bombsite, can accommodate 7,000.

London's greatest minority religion has to serve a number of different, distinct communities, from East London Bangladeshis and north London Turks to the Ahmadi Indians of south London. But the London Central Mosque in Regent's Park retains its place as the most important celebration of Islam in the heart of the city.

HINDUS AND ZOROASTRIANS

Two religions claim to be the oldest in the world: Hinduism and Zoroastrianism. Their north London centres of worship could not be more different.

The **Shri Swaminarayan Hindu Temple** in Neasden appears above the semi-suburban streets like a confectioner's dream: a sugar-white cake with generous cream piping and small flags stuck on top. Suddenly the North Circular, Tescos, Ikea, the whole dreary drudge of North London seems to be a continent away.

Nor is it entirely fanciful to think of this dazzling palace, which has been described as one of London's Seven Wonders, as something from another planet that has arrived out of a grey sky to lift the hearts of a weary population, its doors opening in a great shaft of light to reveal gloriously gaudy gods and release its devout followers to disperse and spread their faith. Of course, the truth is that the impetus was the other way, the local faithful gathering together to raise the temple up to the heavens. And if its appearance was not instant, it was still pretty quick. What was then the largest active Hindu *mandir*, or temple, to be built outside India was completed in less than three years after the foundation was laid in 1992.

The story of its building is a real testament of

faith, which began twenty years earlier with Idi Amin's expulsion of Asians in Uganda that brought Hindus of mainly Gujarati origin to London. At first, they used existing buildings for their temple: an Islington church, then a warehouse in Neasden. The guru who inspired them to improve on their make-do accommodation was Brahmaswarup Yogiji Maharaj, the spiritual leader of Bochasanwasi Shri Akshar Purushottam Swaminarayan Sanstha (BAPS).

Yogiji Maharaj was an advocate of temple building. As spiritual head of BAPS he had opened five *mandirs* in East Africa, and on a visit to England shortly before Amin's edict, he prophesied that a traditional stone *mandir* would soon be built in London, too. It would continue a process started by BAPS' founder Bhagwan Swaminarayan, who between 1822 and 1829 had overseen the building of seven three-pinnacled (*shikharbaddh*) *mandirs*. These provided the model for Neasden, which Yogiji Maharaj lived just long enough to see completed.

The 1.5-acre site was a lorry park next to the warehouse that until then had been used as a temple. A record-breaking 4,500 tons of concrete laid the foundations in a single day. One hundred full-time workers were employed and there were a thousand full-time volunteers. Limestone for the facing came from Bulgaria, marble for the interior from Italy and India, and 26,000 blocks of stone were shaped by some 1,500 masons and sculptors in a specially built workshop in India, and then shipped to London to be pieced together in a giant 3D jigsaw puzzle. Unlike the temples of Mammon, temples to deities are designed to last for as near eternity as man can make them, and this one is built to stand for a thousand years. No ferrous metals or any other corrosive material has been used in its construction. In fact the central cantilevered dome is said to be one of the largest ever built in the UK without using iron or steel.

Next to the *mandir* is the Haveli, which does for wood what the *mandir* does for stone. Again, based on traditional designs, it has a timber balcony along the length of its front, supported by wooden pillars, and carved with geometric patterns and garlands of flowers. The Haveli is the business end of the temple, the cultural centre and main entrance, which leads to the *ashram*, where some sixteen monks, called *sardhus*, are in residence.

In India a *haveli* is built around an open courtyard, but British weather requires glass roofs for the double courtyard reception area. Here oak panelled walls, pillars and ceilings are crafted with patterns and figures, once more by artisans in India, some 150 of them. More than 200 oaks cut down in Devon were replaced with 2,000 saplings, and teak was imported from Burma. Shoes are removed before entering this spacious reception hall, where there is a shop to buy incense sticks, plus a selection of souvenirs that are in cheerful red and gold. Beyond it is a prayer hall that can accommodate 3,000. The Haveli also contains a gymnasium, medical centre, bookstall, and conference rooms.

The *mandir* is reached through a passage to the left beside an open courtyard. Beneath it, on the ground floor, an exhibition explains the religion, which is based on the idea of reincarnation, has more than 300 gods and claims to be the world's oldest religion. Upstairs is the main, domed temple room, where services are held throughout the day, and visitors are free to attend. At these times shrine doors are removed to reveal the images of gods, while behind the main shrine are the *murtis*, life-sized images of the three former leaders of the sect, plus the living one, Pramukh Swami Maharaj. The founding guru, Swaminarayan, has a temple room of his own, and followers circumambulate his shrine, their right arms raised towards him, chanting his name.

The saffron-robed monks who look after the *murtis* have served their term in India, first for two years to see if this is what they really want: they must, for example, learn not to catch a woman's eye. Then for five years they study world religions as well as their own.

Perhaps recruits to their calling will come from among the 500 or so pupils of the Swaminarayan School opposite. The premises of the former Sladebrook High School were snapped up by BAPS after it closed in 1990, to become Europe's first independent Hindu school. As well as teaching Hindu culture, it follows the national curriculum, charges around £9,000 a year and scores high in national league tables.

Across the street is a car park, where visitors to the *mandir* must leave their cameras and bags. The supermarket and restaurant at the far end of the car park are in the warehouse where the previous, much more modest Hindu temple stood. Full of Indian delights, the shop sells vegetables from the sub-continent, as well as piles of boxes of crisps and 'savouries'. There is a takeaway counter, with bright coloured sweets, ice creams and snacks, and the Shayona Restaurant serving Sattvic cuisine. Although this involves no meat or fish, and no strong tastes such as garlic or onion, and there is no alcohol to be had, it has melted the hearts and gladdened the stomachs of some the most hard-boiled London restaurant critics.

Visitors to the **Zoroastrian Centre** half a dozen miles west of the Neasden temple opposite Rayners Lane tube station in Alexandra Avenue have to settle for one of any number of mainly Asian takeaways.

Zoroastrianism is a monotheistic, Indo-Iranian religion, and like Mithraism it was once thought of as a rival to Christianity, though it did not arrive in London until the 19th century. Also claiming to be the oldest religion in the world, Zoroastrianism may have started around 12,000 years ago, and for more than a millennium, from 650BC to AD600 it was the official religion of the Persians who followed the teaching of its principal prophet, Zoroastra, or Zarathusa. It is not a proselytising religion, but it has survived.

Britain's best-known Zoroastrian was Freddie Mercury of Queen, who was born into a family of Parsis in Mumbai (Bombay) in 1946. Although initiated into the religion at the age of eight, he did not practice it in later life and it was not until his funeral, conducted entirely in the Avestan language of ancient Iran, that this fact became widely known.

Zoroastrians have little by way of ceremony and idolatrous clutter. Their relatively simple beliefs are expressed in the purity of fire and water. They don't go in for celibacy or fasting and are encouraged to enjoy life, to use the brain that Ahura Mazda, the Wise One, has given them to dispel ignorance and blind faith. For their initiation, followers are given a cord (*kusti*) to wrap three times around a long white cotton shirt (*sudreh*) to emphasise their three basic tenets: good words, good thoughts, good deeds.

There are around 8,000 Zoroastrians in Britain,

most of whom live in London, which has the oldest diaspora community in the West. Their headquarters in a former cinema in Harrow is the only place of Zoroastrian worship in Europe. The Zoroastrian Centre is run by the charitable Zoroastrian Trust Funds of Europe, which was set up in 1861 by a charismatic cotton trader from Mumbai, Dadabhai Naoroji, who was also an ordained Zoroastrian priest. Entering parliament as Liberal Member for Finsbury Central in 1882, he took the oath on his copy of *Khorda Avesta*, his religion's bible. He was Britain's first Asian MP.

The organisation that he started has existed ever since, and in 1980, following the diaspora caused by the Iranian revolution, it took over the abandoned Grade II* listed **Grosvenor Cinema** in Harrow, a beautiful Art Deco building designed by Frank Bromige that had once been a temple to the silver screen. Now its inner sanctum is the *setayash gah*, the fire temple where sacred flames flicker.

In 2012 Almut Hintze, a pastor's daughter from Heidelberg, took up the post of Professor of Zoroastrianism at London University's School of Oriental and African Studies (SOAS). Sponsored by the Iranian philanthropists Mehraban and Faridoon Zartoshty, the Zartoshty Chair in the Department of Religious Studies is the world's first fully-endowed university position in Zoroastrianism.

SALVATION IN SOUTHWARK

Southwark, once the playground of London, has dabbled with debauchery, it's true, but it also has a deep religious soul. In Shakespeare's day this is where people went to theatres, to watch bear baiting, to drink and visit bawdy houses, but it is also where the pilgrims began their journey in Chaucer's *Canterbury Tales*. In the much-enlarged modern borough of more than a quarter of a million people, church attendance has risen by an around 25 percent since 2005. The Christian God is served in many ways, from the silence of the Quaker Meeting House to the ecstasy of Evangelicals, from the hymns of Charles Wesley to the insistent beat of world music. The rituals are as varied as the temples, which include the Salvation Army headquarters and training college, the largest non-conformist church in London and the highest concentration of new Black Majority Churches (nBMCs) in Britain. It is also the only London borough to support both an Anglican and a Catholic cathedral.

For Anglicans, the high point is **St Saviour's Cathedral** by London Bridge. A solid, squat building with a fanfare of flags on a battlemented tower fit for a jousting tournament, it pops up in the foreground of many panoramas of the capital seen from the south across the Thames. Said to be the earliest surviving Gothic church in the city, it has a peal of twelve bells, a fine organ, a long choral tradition and five services every day. Until 1877 this former medieval Augustinian priory church of St Mary Overie was in the see of the Bishop of Winchester whose ruined palace stands nearby. In 1905, after a Victorian makeover, it was designated the cathedral of the new diocese of Southwark.

Visitors to Borough Market who are tempted to drift into St Saviour's are caught by the £4 entrance fee, the price to be paid for looking round an ancient church that clings to its heritage as well as any visitor attraction. Here, it is quickly pointed out, John Harvard, founder of the American university, was baptised; and though buried miles away in Stratford-upon-Avon, William Shakespeare has a fine memorial. His brother Edmund is somewhere among several thespians interred beneath the flagstone floor.

St George's Roman Catholic Cathedral, by contrast, can be entered freely, is off the tourist map, and is not very old. Nevertheless, it is rewarding for the great humbling silence it contains. But the space responds well to music, too, and the nave's high neo-Gothic arches have rung to a variety of hymns ancient and modern, from plainsong to Latin American beats. Just over a mile from Southwark Cathedral, it was built just as soon as the Emancipation Act of 1829 allowed, founded through the energies of Father Thomas Doyle, who is credited as being the first priest in Britain since the Reformation to introduce public devotions to the Virgin Mary. The white Cotswold limestone stretches heavenward to the designs of the great Catholic architect Augustus Welby Pugin, although much of his work, in particular the high altar, was devastated by a wartime incendiary bomb.

St George's is airy, cool and, for a Catholic church, sparse, perhaps because it slipped out of the limelight when John Francis Bentley's much more lavish neo-Byzantine **Westminster Cathedral** began to take shape across the river in Victoria Street towards the end of the 19th century. Glistening with mosaics and marble fit for a patriarch, the mother church of the Catholics of England and Wales attracts a wealthier congregation than St George's, which serves a large immigrant population. In the south aisle, among the cupboard doors of the confessionals, is a recent shrine to St Francesca Cabrini, an Italian missionary and frequent visitor, who was born in the year that the Cathedral was dedicated. Through her work as founder of the worldwide Sisters of the Sacred Heart of Jesus, she became the patron saint of immigrants.

"Today, approximately one in 35 people worldwide are on the move," a note in the church says, *"enough to make up the fifth largest nation on earth."*

Among the many who have been on the move is a large local Latin American population, and every Sunday at one o'clock a Mass is held in Spanish.

Although Southwark is the first London borough formally to classify its residents as Latin American, there is a distinct lack of Latin fervour at the **London Metropolitan Tabernacle**. This is the outstanding temple opposite one of the bastions of the Latino community, the Elephant and Castle Shopping Centre. The Tabernacle's rich ochre stones, with a portico of six giant Corinthian pillars and a low,

174

sloping pediment, have made it a steadfast anchor in a neglected area undergoing an ambitious £3 billion regeneration programme that will pull down the shopping centre and drive out many recent arrivals.

Behind the Tabernacle's timeless façade there is a 1950s meeting hall, rebuilt after wartime bombing, a light and tidy space with a dais on which the lone figure of the pastor conducts the service and delivers a faultless, lengthy and deliberately uncharismatic sermon. He is Dr Peter Masters, upright in a business suit, who has led the congregation since 1970 and become a major figure in the movement, attracting regular attendances of 4–500, a number that might tempt other clergies into the sin of covetousness.

The Tabernacle's services are austere. Bible readings, hymns and prayers bookend the sermon. There is neither liturgy nor choir, no dialogue with the congregation, no responses. A wide mix of ages and ethnicities attend, headphones provide simultaneous translation in Spanish, Portuguese, Chinese, Korean and French, and there is live streaming on the web. An unseen organ accompanies the hymns, which are heartily sung, and rendered in sign language for the deaf. Dr Masters is an enemy of the 'aesthetics' that detract from the Bible's message, and he is anxious to point out that the organ is for accompaniment only, and should not itself be seen as an enrichment of worship.

Charles Haddon Spurgeon, for whom the Tabernacle was built in 1861, would not have stood for an organ. The building then was a much larger place. Spurgeon was a phenomenon. When he was just twenty-two he preached to an unprecedented 10,000 in the nearby Surrey Gardens Music Hall, during which seven were killed in the crush. Based on the Music Hall, the Tabernacle had two tiers of galleries and could seat five thousand, plus a thousand standing. Spurgeon's sermons, published weekly, were best-sellers. Dr Masters, in his footsteps, publishes his on line, and has a wealth of material in print, too.

Spurgeon was a contemporary of the Salvation Army founder William Booth who started his mission in the East End. Both saw the light in their teens, and Spurgeon would commend Booth for "stirring the masses of London". One of Booth's ambitions was to build a 'University of Humanity' to train his cadets for their work, but it was only after his death that his son, Bramwell, managed to purchase a large plot of land for the purpose on the hillside opposite what is now Denmark Hill station in Camberwell. For the **William Booth Memorial Training College** they looked to their own Architects Office, set up in 1870 and one of the oldest in London when it finally closed in 2002. Gordon and Viner, about whom little seems to be known, were the in-house architects, but the college needed to be something special, so Sir Giles Gilbert Scott was brought in to design its exterior. This had to echo the flavour of the Salvation Army's other 'citadels' which often had battlemented parapets and flanking towers.

Unsurprisingly, the architect of Bankside Power Station used brick as the principal building material, though these were bought cheaply from the Netherlands and are just 2in (50mm) in height, an inch short of the traditional brick, giving the whole building a distinctive look. A central tower with a huge cross that lights up at night is a foretaste of the Tate Modern chimney, while the Gothic stone entrance and narrow, leaded windows seem to belong to a grand country house.

When the building opened in 1928, the centenary of William Booth's birth, there were nine houses in the grounds, where 500 unmarried cadets lived in segregated 'cells' during their six-months' training. Today, the courses last two years, and there are only fifty or so cadets, all with families. The meeting hall used for services is not open to the public, though there is a small heritage centre on the third floor, reached by an oak-panelled lift filmed for *Poirot* as the lift in the Belgian detective's thirties flat.

Salvation lies thick on the ground in nearby Peckham where half of more than 250 'new black majority churches' in Southwark are to be found. The community is largely Nigerian and Ghanaian, Caribbean, too, and this makes commercial Rye Lane vibrant on any day of the week. Saviour's Hair Salon, Divine Money Foreign Exchange and the God Bless Restaurant are typical of shop signs that catch the eye. There are many established missionaries and churches tucked behind and above the shops and wondrous are their names, from Beneficial Veracious at the Christ Church Miracle Centre to the Latter-Rain Outpouring Church. In the Bussey Building in Copeland Industrial Park, where cricket bats were once manufactured, no fewer than a dozen churches operate from the many rooms that are also occupied by young creatives. The demand for places to hold religious gatherings outstrips available space, not least because there are many objections to licences on the grounds of noise and parking space.

On Sundays Rye Lane is a catwalk of gorgeous robes, headdresses, shawls, scarves and hats that make Western attire seem dull. Hair is beautifully sleek, in braids and twists, jewellery is chunky and sparkling, and the children are in their cutest party clothes. Women and girl choristers wear white bonnets that look a little like chefs' hats, and *santeros* and *santeras* float by like the departed come back to life. Music and singing pours out of unexpected corners, and in the most exotic services chanting will lead to trances of ecstasy.

At the modern 'temple' of the **Universal Church of the Kingdom of God** in Rye Lane smartly dressed young adherents urge passers-by to improve their personal relationships by enrolling in their Love School. This 'neo-Pentecostal' organisation has filled Wembley Arena and claims 1.5 million followers worldwide, though its leader, Brazilian billionaire Edir Macedo, has been charged with tax-evasion. He preaches against pop and rap music as the music of Satan, and is reported to have convinced children at services that they are possessed by the devil. In Ealing, the UCKG pastor Álvaro Lima was preparing to cast out the devil from eight-year old Victoria Climbié on the day she died of abuse and neglect by her guardians. Elsewhere there have been reports of 'miracle babies' and child trafficking.

From saints to snake oil salesmen, the worshippers and faiths in the Christian churches and temples of Southwark are as broad as the old River Jordan in full spate. Even those who believe that religion is a personal matter between man and God, without the need of any hierarchy or bricks and mortar, have been affected by Southwark's spiritual spark. At the age of eight, the poet and mystic William Blake had a vision of angels on Peckham Rye.

THE LAST WORD

There comes a time for all men to leave Mammon behind to face their god penniless and naked. Some slip quietly away to turn to dust and ashes, others have one final spending spree on a monument they hope might bring redemption and immortality.

London's main cemeteries are full of such monuments, stone tombs and temples set about with symbols and angels in that drama of death in which the Victorians, in particular, indulged. A taste for mausoleums had initially come from India and the examples of the Moghuls, though the word 'mausoleum' was given to the world by King Mausolus of Caria, whose magnificent 4th-century BC tomb was known as the Mausoleum of Halicarnassus, modern Bodrum in Turkey. This was one of the Seven Wonders of the Ancient World, and its plundered remnants, including colossal statues of what were thought to be Mausolus himself and his queen, Artemesia, were acquired in 1859 by the British Museum where they can still be seen.

It was in Victorian times when the fashion was for Classical and Gothic that municipal cemeteries were established around the capital to take the overflow from churchyards that were beyond bursting point. **Kensal Green Cemetery**, the first to open, in 1833, decided on pure Greek Revival mortuary chapels: Doric for the Anglicans, Ionic for the Dissenters. The **Brompton Cemetery** went for a pastiche of St Peter's in Rome, while **Highgate Cemetery,** where plots can still be bought for around £9,000, took the pharaonic route on its Egyptian Avenue.

Karl Marx is the celebrity of Highgate Cemetery. His much photographed bust by Laurence Bradshaw in the East Cemetery, which can be freely visited, rises above a tomb that continues to urge the workers of the world to unite. The older, West Cemetery runs tours by apppointment, and here at the highest point in Highgate, above the Egyptian Avenue and surrounded by the Circle of Lebanon, is the richest tomb, the last resting place of the financier Julius Beer. With a stepped pyramid roof inspired by the Mausoleum of Halicarnassus, this is the summit of the cemetery both in elevation and grandeur.

Beer had been born without means in Frankfurt, and made enough money on the London Stock Exchange to buy the *Observer* newspaper. The tomb was made in Portland stone by Italian craftsmen with fine bronze doors by the Bromsgrove Guild. It was built for Beer's daughter, Ada, who died of consumption aged six in 1875, five years before the financier's own death. A statue of Ada being lifted up by an angel, sculpted by Henry Armstead who created many of the figures on the Albert Memorial, is beneath the interior blue and gold dome. Beer and his wife Thyrza, brother Arnold and son Frederick are all interred here.

Frederick took over the *Observer* on the death of his father, and his wife, Rachel Sassoon, became the first woman editor of a national newspaper, later purchasing the *Sunday Times*, which she also edited.

She was from the Iraqi Sassoon family, aunt of the poet Siegfried to whom she gave a living. She was buried in the Sassoon Mausoleum in Brighton, a building of Indo-Saracenic design with a distinctive copper, tented roof that has since given up all solemnity, being used as a warehouse, air-raid shelter, pub and finally a burlesque venue, the Proud Cabaret.

The architect of the Beer Mausoleum was John Oldrid Scott, grandson of George Gilbert Scott, who three years before the death of young Ada Beer had built a large mortuary chapel in the South Metropolitan Cemetery in South London, now called the **West Norwood Cemetery**. It was commissioned to commemorate the death of another young person, Augustus Ralli, an Eton student who succumbed to rheumatic fever at the age of sixteen. Augustus was the son of Stephanos Ralli, from the spectacularly successful Ralli family of Chios in Greece who had come to London in 1821 during the diaspora caused by the Greek War of Independence, in which the island had seen a massacre of its population. The Rallis quickly built a business that stretched from America to India, where they still operate, and at their height are said to have employed 40,000 staff. They funded much of the London activity of the growing Hellenic community, including the building of **St Sofia Greek Orthodox Cathedral** in Bayswater, which was also designed by John Oldrid Scott.

The cathedral's first stone was laid by Stephanos Ralli, and when his schoolboy son died he asked if he could build the mortuary chapel in the cemetery plot in the South Metropolitan Cemetery, which the Hellenic community, with the Rallis' help, had acquired. Named St Stephen's after its benefactor, the chapel is based on the Parthenon, with Archangel Gabriel occupying the tympanum and a frieze with scenes from the Bible.

Eighteen of the monuments in the Greek Orthodox plot on the lower ground of the northeast side of the cemetery are Grade II and Grade II* listed by English Heritage, many of them in Classical style. The tomb of Panayis Athanase Vagliano, founder of the National Library of Greece and 'the father of Greek shipping', is a replica of the Tower of the Winds in Athens, while the main Ralli tomb by George Edmund Street, architect of the Gothic Law Courts in the Strand, is modelled on a Lycian tomb, and the mausoleum of Eustratios Ralli is by Edward M. Barry, who completed his father's work on the Palace of Westminster.

A further fifty monuments in the cemetery are listed, less than half the number in Kensal Green. Much has been lost. Pressure on space caused Lambeth Council to compulsory purchase the cemetery in 1965 and demolish several thousand monuments, including some that were listed. Those that remain can only hint at why it was once known as 'the Millionaire's Cemetery'. Covering a hill and landscaped for people's enjoyment, it was laid out by one of the cemetery's directors, William Tite, who had moved away from the Classical style he employed at the Royal Exchange. Here he created the first Gothic cemetery in Britain, and though it was designed along the lines of a pleasure garden, it would help to confirm the link between the word 'Gothic' with the horrors of death.

Tite is interred in the catacombs that he himself designed, with a hydraulic lift for the coffins. The catacombs lie beneath the modern crematorium built on his mortuary chapels that were pulled down after being damaged in the war. Before he passed away he created a monumental Gothic spire for James William Gilbart, who had "enjoyed for 50 years the Science of Banking". The first manager of the pioneering London and Westminster joint stock bank, for which William Tite was a director and architect, Gilbart "died with the satisfaction of knowing that he left one of the largest and most powerful Joint Stock Banks in the Kingdom".

Among other familiar names of the departed from the temples of London are Charles Spurgeon, charismatic preacher of the Metropolitan Tabernacle, Charles Driver of Abbey Mills and Crossness pumping stations, and Horace Jones, Architect and Surveyor to the City of London who built Tower Bridge as well as Billingsgate, Leadenhall and Smithfield markets, and whose simple slab is covered with brambles. Beneath another solid piece of granite is Queen Victoria's favourite builder Thomas Cubitt, who extended Buckingham Palace, moved Nash's Marble Arch for the Great Exhibition and built much of Belgravia, where a pub and restaurant named after him celebrates his many achievements. More joyous are a pair of red terracotta mausoleums designed by the landscape architect Harold Peto for the final resting places of the Lambeth pottery manufacturer John Doulton and sugar baron Sir Henry Tate, founder of the Tate Gallery.

There are no signs that the architects of London today are preparing stylish contemporary mausoleums for themselves or their wealthy patrons. Some such structures have appeared in Italy and in the US, so it might not be long before they catch on here. In the meantime, all that architects need to do in this city of continually rising towers is adopt the words on the tablet to Sir Christopher Wren in the crypt of **St Paul's Cathedral**: *Lector, si monumentum requiris, circumspic*:

'Reader, if you seek my monument, look around you...'

Buildings and architects

INDEX

INDEX